A Stroll in my Moccasins

A Stroll in my Moccasins

AUDREY E PAYNE

A catalogue record for this book is available from the National Library of Australia

Publishing Details:
ISBN: 978-0-6485795-0-2 (Paperback)
ISBN: 979-0-6485795-1-9 (Hardback)

Publisher: Wise Owl Books
Book enquiries to albanyaud@gmail.com

Cover / Interior Layout: Pickawoowoo Publishing Group
Editing: Eddie Albrecht, Pickawoowoo Publishing Group
Printed and channel distribution: Lightning Source / Ingram

Contents

Acknowledgements

Memory can play tricks, and memoir by its very name indicates subjectivity and likely bias. That said, I have tried not to twist the truth as I saw it, apart from re-inventing or omitting a few names. Conversations are in character.

I am grateful to friends who encouraged me to record some of my life story and suffered my initial efforts. My thanks go to Rhuwina Griffiths who started me off, Sheryl Nostrini whose weekly support kept me going and the Great Southern Writers Group which walked this journey with me.

This book is dedicated to my family and written for my nieces Clare, Faye and Theresa and great nephew Ryan, who carries the genes. It is offered, with some trepidation, to anyone who may like to take a stroll in another's footsteps.

Prologue

Pray, don't find fault with the man that limps,
Or stumbles along the road.
Unless you have worn the moccasins he wears,
Or stumbled beneath the same load.

— MARY T. LATHRAP IN 1895

Moccasins describe soft American Indian shoes with a quiet tread. My life has been a quiet walk with interesting experiences and a few stumbles along the way.

Two strangers approaching one another in the African bush call out, 'Greetings. Where are you coming from?' followed by, 'Where are you going?' People I meet ask, 'Where are you from?' These opening questions that were once so simple to answer, have given me cause for hesitation as life progressed. As a child of Britain's faded colonial past, and I'm just one of many, the answer is complicated. I look and sound English, but I'm not. Although I now say I'm Australian, I am met with the same curiosity: where are you from?

It's a good question, but one that is difficult to answer briefly. Perhaps, 'Where have you been, or where are you going?' are the more important questions. Where I end up is the most unexpected part of my life journey.

This is a conversation we might have as we stroll along together, and it entwines some of my spiritual walk.

One

FAMILY FACTS AND FABLES

Pushed into life,
in Scotland's Fife,
where no bombs fall
or sirens call,
I'm kept happy,
just change my nappy!
*

Loved and pampered
off we scampered
south by train,
then up again,
following Father who, I'm sure
would rather be home
and not at war.

I sat in my small garden, removed my clerical collar and sipped my cup of tea. Two grey doves sat at peace in the slender branches of my silver birch tree, and the intense scent of sweet peas contradicted the delicate hues of their flowers. It could have been England, but it wasn't. I was content here in the warmth of the afternoon sun that reminded me summer was approaching. It was Sunday, November 11th, Armistice Day, when we remember past wars and those who fought and died in them. It was a day for me to cast my mind back to my loved late father and the stories he told us of his World War II experiences. One in particular was memorable and well documented and I begin my life story with it. It happened in 1943, the year I was born. Being born during wartime is not the best timing, but it wasn't up to me.

1943. A velvet night sky cloaked the flight of the unarmed aircraft above the Skagerrak, the narrow stretch of water separating Norway and Denmark. Both coastlines were flanked by powerful flak batteries and several units of Luftwaffe fighter planes. In 1943, this was the danger hotspot for the British Overseas Airways Corporation (BOAC) return flight from neutral Sweden to the east coast of Scotland. Captain Gilbert Rae (Gibbie) and Radio Officer James Payne (Jimmy) craned their necks to scan the skies, their senses tingling on high alert.

'Gerry at 2 o'clock!...and 10!' yelled Jimmy into his flying mask.

'Here we go again,' Gibbie's response was calm.

Jimmy gripped the flight plans, knowing what was to come. Gibbie pushed hard on the joystick, and their heart rates rose in unison with the speed of the plane's steep dive seawards. Tracers from the flak batteries lit the sky as the German fighters urged their two German Fw 190s to match the Mosquito's rapid dive. Jimmie watched the altimeter: 23,000 feet…22,000…21,000, 20… 19… 18. The plane began to shake. It wasn't a good time to remember its structure was essentially plywood. Jimmy's ears were deaf to the shriek of the engine. He was severely shaken in body and mind as Gibbie straightened up in the layer of mist at 10,000 feet. [1]

You'd think we'd be used to this by now. Thank God I'm with the best pilot of a good bunch. Jimmy's thoughts settled on his family waiting for him in the ancient Scottish city of St Andrews; Hilda, his lovely wife, and his two daughters, 18-month-old Frances and baby Audrey. He hoped he'd survive this war to see them grow up. He did, but sadly, Gibbie didn't.

At home, Hilda busied herself with the children and household chores, washing, ironing, play and afternoon walks. Hilda's childrearing skills came

---

1 https://www.pprune.org/archive/index.php/t-383856.html

from being fourth in a family of twelve and through being the nanny for a clergyman's family. That was before she married Jimmy, whom she called Jim. She pegged the last of the nappies on the line in their small back garden and she waved to her neighbour. The longer Jim was away, the more her anxiety increased.

I hate this waiting, but I suppose I'm not the only wife waiting and worrying at home, she told herself. She tried not to remember the times she had waited for her fiancé Gordon, until that time etched in her heart when he didn't return. He was a pilot and an early casualty of this awful war.

In St Andrews, people lived in comparative safety while most of the men were away fighting. The women of the neighbourhood watched Father's comings and goings and assumed Mother had it easy with a husband who frequently returned home for days at a time. Most of their husbands seldom, or never came back. What they didn't know was that our Father was not at all safe and Mother never knew when, or if he would return. Mother couldn't respond to their resentment, but all was made clear when Father was awarded the civilian honour of an MBE (Member of the Order of the British Empire) in October 1943. This award was for, '*Courage of a high order over an extended period in flying unarmed aircraft on the civil wartime service between the United Kingdom and Stockholm.*'

Gilbert Rae (left) and James S.W. Payne, MBE

Frances and I were the least anxious ones in our family during those years. We were born in the small maternity hospital in St Andrews. Frances arrived in 1941 and I came one summer's morning almost two years later. I assume that my being born at 8.30am is what put me off breakfast for the rest of my life. However, my otherwise healthy appetite grew me into a podgy blonde with a happy disposition.

As a shy younger child, my early life was marked by the decisions of others. Later I opted to make my own choices with varying results. My Christian faith began with infant baptism in Saint Andrews Episcopal Church where I was christened Audrey Elizabeth. This second name dated many women of my generation, being that of the popular young Princess. Our parents' nurture proved invaluable as our lives unfolded in unexpected ways.

A birthplace in St Andrews does not make me Scottish, any more than being born in the golf mecca of the world makes me a golfer. Father was the one who gave me Scottish ancestry and my DNA lacks a golfing strand.

My ancestry is not remarkable and its relevance to my story is limited to my parents and grandparents. My memories emerge, sometimes out of sequence, and weave in and out of their lives.

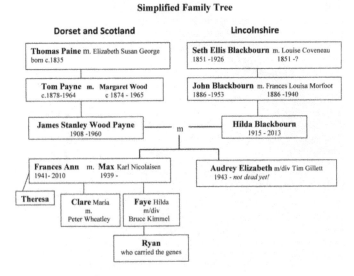

Simplified Family Tree

Three generations of our family tree

Jim and Hilda – my parents

My parents met through mutual friends in the early years of the war and married in July 1940. Before war was declared, Mother was in love with an older pilot, Gordon. Sadly, Gordon was killed in 1939, only days before Christmas. It's possible she married Father on the rebound, but he loved her, and she grew to return his love. Father once told me that he'd been putting his shoes on one morning when a thought popped into his head, *I'd better ask Hilda to marry me before someone else does.* His timing was right and as it turned out they were well suited and happily married for 18 years.

Mother's influence on my life was subtle but my Father was the more significant person in my early life and I remember him with love and admiration.

Jim was born in 1908 in Scotland and raised in North London. He was endlessly curious and enthusiastic about life, and his only way to see the world was to join the merchant navy. In the 1930s he studied to become a wireless operator in Marconi's radio school and went to sea.

'I spent eleven years trying to get out,' he once told me.

During my childhood, I heard something of the countries he visited and his life at sea as I tagged along with him on his many enthusiasms.

'We had to get out of the St Lawrence River by September, or we'd be iced-in for the winter.' I'd look for a map of Canada.

Father played ice hockey, and as a five-year-old I found his ice skates at the back of a wardrobe and puzzled over them. Maybe he took up ice hockey during one of those ice-bound Canadian winters. Other pieces of information would be dropped into a conversation.

'The women in India didn't stop work when they had babies,' he once told me as we worked on one of his projects. 'They'd just drop out of the work line, have their baby and come back a bit later.'

This comment stayed with me and I wondered if I could expect to do the same in future years.

Before World War II, Father became fascinated with aircraft and wanted to learn to fly. The closest he came was to work with De Havilland Aircraft Company at Hanger Lane Aerodrome in London. This is where the wooden Mosquito light bombers were built. During the war, BOAC employed him as a radio officer, and this was how he became part of BOAC's clandestine war effort.

We were always very proud of Father's war service. Frances wrote a lengthy and well-researched article that tells the story in some detail. It was published in the March 2004 edition of *Aeroplane,* a monthly publication for plane enthusiasts worldwide. In it, she wrote about the incident described earlier.

We loved to hear Father's stories as we grew up, pestering him: 'Tell us another story about the war, Daddy.'

We never tired of hearing about the times they were under attack when he had to swallow the secret information written on rice paper. Because of this story, we happily ate the rice paper under Mother's baked macaroons. Our favourite story was the one where Father and Gilbert were transporting an important escaped Danish physicist in the plane's empty bomb bay. He was secreted on board in Sweden, already dressed in warm flying gear. About an hour and a half into the flight and at 23,000 feet they came under attack from two German Fw 190s. Gilbert immediately did his usual diving manoeuvre of tight spirals to escape into the fog below. After things settled, they called the passenger on the intercom. No response, so Father poked at him through a gap with a small screwdriver. Still no answer. About 20 minutes later a shaky voice came through the intercom: 'Dat vos very funny fife minutes ago!' Their very important passenger had passed out earlier as his oxygen mask dislodged, and the lower altitude revived him. Father received cuts and bruises from the plane's buffeting and was grounded for a while.

Father's war work not only earned him an MBE and a nomination for a Norwegian award, but also a place on Hermann Goering's 'hit list' because of their cargo of vital steel-parts and their persistent evasion of the proudly efficient Luftwaffe. Pilot Gilbert once retaliated in a small but satisfying way as he and Father taxied on the runway at Stockholm's Bromma Airport. Goering was boarding his flight nearby and Gilbert swung the Mosquito into a skid that sent swirling dust over the enemy.

Gilbert was killed when his aeroplane was presumed sabotaged on a return flight from Sweden. It was a blessing for us that Father was not on that flight. The flight crews from Germany and Britain shared the mess hall at Bromma airport, where they also replenished their thermos flasks for the return trip. On a previous trip, there had been an incident and scuffle in the mess room which puzzled both Father and Gilbert at the time. It was possible that it was an attempt to tamper with the British crew's thermos flasks. Gilbert was 26 years old when his flight went down close to the Scottish coast. He had completed 150 return trips to Sweden, and Father who was considered 'the old man' at 35, completed a similar number of trips. The book *The Ball Bearing Run* by Walter Winyard (Corgi Books. 1981, pp. 28) attests to these missions and Father's story, adding that the death of Gilbert and his crew 'brought a mighty sigh of relief in Berlin'. Others of BOAC's brave mission continued to fly.

We would have bathed in our Father's reflected glory if he'd not been such a humble, unassuming man. He never told people he had been decorated for his part in BOAC's little-known contribution to the war effort. Everyone was doing their bit. I was just eating and sleeping and travelling by train through the war-torn cities of the English Midlands to Bristol in the south-west of England, following Father and his war work

My mother, Hilda, delighted in motherhood and brought us up with love, wanting the best for us both. I was pleased to be able to thank her in later life for her early care. She was intelligent with a sense of adventure and humour that was only seen by family and those she knew well. She went on to live into her 99th year and never looked her age. She suffered low self-esteem and was prone to anxiety which emerged later in life as depression. This may have been the result of her wartime experiences, violence and loss of loved ones. Her sense of natural justice was acute and she was often heard to complain, 'It's not fair.' We came to laugh with her about this and I threatened to put it on her gravestone, which I did, along with another loving statement.

Mother's big regret in life was missing out on a scholarship to attend the local grammar school. She blamed this on her being the fourth child in a family of six boys and six girls, and she was probably right. As a result, she left school at 14 to work in her father's green grocery shop and help with her siblings and the housework. We grew up with tales of her family's life and would pester her for stories of 'the olden days'. Life was frugal in their large family, but they had fun among the usual sibling rivalries. They each played a musical instrument, Mother's was a violin. She bemoaned the constant arrival of more babies, telling us that she once complained to her mother, sobbing, 'Why can't the doctor take the babies to Connie's house? She hasn't got any brothers or sisters.'

Father, Mother, Frances and me.

I note that my parents stopped at two children. My unintentional contribution to the planet and our well-populated family tree has been to *not* add to the count. Mother's time as a nanny taught her some approaches to child-rearing that led to Frances and I being raised in a similar way. These included routines, a quiet environment for sleep and a system of discipline involving one warning before a threatened punishment was meted out. The penalty was usually the withdrawal of a treat or being sent out of the room. Mother was a well organised and tidy person with a smart taste in clothes. Frances and I both inherited her organisational abilities if not her love of routine. Frances inherited a larger portion of her neatness, style and 'presence'. Hilda's sense of humour included a strong sense of the ridiculous and these qualities continued in following generations, although I'm told I have an added dollop of my grandfather and father's dry wit.

The Blessing of Grandparents

The influence of grandparents goes unnoticed in our childhood years, but snippets of family stories and traits are retained and can emerge in later life. This is how it has been for me and I see bits of them in myself, my sister and our cousins.

Mother's parents – John and Frances Blackbourn

Mother's father, John, came from a long line of solid Lincolnshire yeomen (freemen) and early engineers who farmed around the ancient Saxon village of Leasingham, 16 miles south of Lincoln. As yeomen, these ancestors were obliged to fight under the banner of the local squire in return for their land leases. The village is listed in the Domesday Book of AD 1086 and parts of the first church building in the village date back to AD 1100. It's dedicated to Saint Andrew, which is a strange connection to my birthplace and christening centuries later. The Leasingham church records hold some of our family baptisms and the graveyard contains some family graves from the 18th century. The Blackbourn branch of the family moved closer to the cathedral city of Lincoln, possibly in the late 1800s, around the time of the industrial revolution. Lincolnshire mechanised early as their farms were so large. It's likely that some family men were employed in making the first army tanks at Foster's, Lincoln's foundry. Foster's produced continuous track tractors for farmers working on Lincolnshire's rich agricultural land.

Granddad Lincoln, as we called him, missed out on engineering training because the family money ran out. Instead, he owned a greengrocer's shop in the city of Lincoln. His good education led to his being known as 'that Italian grocer' because he painted a Latin motto on the basket in front of his delivery bicycle. Sadly, no one remembers what it said and maybe that's just as well. He liked a joke.

Granddad Lincoln met my grandmother, Frances Moorfoot (spelt Morfoot in some records) when he was walking home and knocked on a farmhouse door to ask for a glass of water, or so the story goes. He was seventeen and she sixteen, and Granddad decided there and then he would marry her. She was a tall, elegant woman and a milliner, often whirling into the family sitting room wearing a refashioned hat to demand, 'How do you like this one?' She coined the phrase, 'A little bit of plain red and yellow,' and this became our family's description for anything tastelessly gaudy. Her mother's maiden name was Coveneau, which suggests French origins and maybe accounts for the sense of style that ran through the women of the family. This part of our ancestry I leave for others to investigate.

Granddad Lincoln was a rotund, happy man. Mother would tell us how he'd sit in his chair after a busy day and chat with his many friends. He sat with a glass of ale balanced precariously on his protruding stomach, and both wobbled dangerously with every rumbling laugh. Granddad died when I was about ten and Grandma died during my infancy. I only knew them through the family fables shared by my Mother and some aunts. I spent more time with my Father's parents.

Father's parents – Tom and Margaret Payne

I knew my Father's parents well during my childhood. Both Tom and Margaret's family backgrounds were agricultural, and when Tom retired they returned to live where he grew up in Dorset. Studland is a heritage-listed seaside village on the coast of Dorset and has been home to many generations of the Payne family. Lacking a more imaginative differentiation between my grandparents, we referred to one pair as Grandma and Granddad Lincoln and the other as Grandma and Granddad Studland.

Grandparents Tom and Margaret Payne

Tom Payne was a strong upright man of average height and lean build, the youngest in a family of seven. As a young man he was with the British in South Africa during the Boer War. Family tradition says he served under Lord Baden-Powell who established the South African Constabulary. We know Granddad rode horses in South Africa and his discharge papers show he served from 1901 to 1906 as Constable Tom Payne, Number 6212. The papers are marked Heidelberg, Cape Colony, and his service reference says he was 'a very hard working and responsible man' with very good conduct and character. During his service he received regular service medals; the Queen's South Africa Medal and Clasp, Cape Colony, Orange Free State and Transvaal, and the King's Medal SA 1902-1906. I doubt he was embroiled in the Boer War as a scout because historical records show they were brutal, and I knew my grandfather as a mild-mannered, gentle man. Baden-Powell was not well liked or respected around that time. Coincidentally, Baden-Powell ended his days in Kenya (East Africa) where I spent most of my childhood.

What our family stories fail to tell is just how Tom met Margaret. Perhaps it was at a dance or maybe at church. What we do know is that Tom, scout or not, had 'scouted out' a good wife. Tom and his new wife returned to England in 1907, and Tom was transferred to the Hampstead Division of the London Metropolitan Police. He worked there until he retired to Studland in 1932. His discharge papers note he was given a full pension and his conduct was exemplary. Good on you, Granddad.

Constable Tom Payne, Hampstead.

Margaret Wood was born in Midlothian, formerly the county of Edinburghshire in south-east Scotland. Her forebears were independent agricultural workers providing seasonal labour teams across the lower border counties. Our tartans include those of the Graham and Stuart clans, making it likely that previous generations came down from the Highlands during the clearances of the 1800s. These clearances were the forced evictions of the Highland crofters by the government of the day to take control of the land for sheep grazing. This policy was also intended to destroy the traditional clan system. Over time, many Highlanders migrated to the Scottish Lowlands or tried their luck overseas.

There were some good singers in our family line and this trait emerges in every generation. Father was a boy soprano and people would come some distance to hear him sing at the church Evensong.

Grandma Studland was a cook, and a good one, having honed her skills 'below stairs' in a country household. I didn't inherit this culinary talent or enthusiasm, as many friends will attest. Grandma travelled with the family to South Africa during the Boer War of the early 1900s, and it was there she met and married Tom Payne and returned with him to England. London was quite a change for a Scottish lass, but Grandma made a good home, a happy marriage and no doubt fed the family well. Old photos show Margaret as a short, plain but smiling woman of neat, stocky appearance with bobbed, straight brown hair that sported a fairer streak above her left brow. I inherited this same streak of hair, perhaps as compensation for not getting a wave, let alone a curl.

Tom and Margaret had twins who did not live long (so I was told) and four surviving children – Tom, James, Hilda and Alec, who all grew up as Londoners. Grandma must have returned to Scotland in 1908 because that is where their second son, my Father, was born and named James Stanley Wood Payne. The story is that she chose his name, but Granddad changed it on the way to register the birth. I think I may have inherited his form of passive resistance when up against a stronger personality. I hope I have learnt to be more assertive with age. Grandma was certainly the boss in her quiet way. Granddad with his mischievous sense of humour would be reprimanded by her whenever one of his saucy ditties went too far.

'Every little helps, the fly said….' he would begin.

'Dad!' she would warn him in her soft accent, giving him The Look.

It was some years before I discovered the last part was '…as it piddled in the sea.' Father inherited The Look. It was enough to keep Frances and me in check in our early years. 'That's far enough!' it said. As an eight-year-old I once countered it with a wink and got away with it, but only the once.

Granddad Tom would disappear behind a haze of smoke in his corner of the sitting room near the 'wireless' and puff away on his pipe during *The Archers*, a daily drama of country life. The scent of his tobacco permeated the house and I began to associate pipe tobacco with a sense of love and comfort. I learned to fill his pipe, and he would prod the leaves into the bowl with his stained thumb before striking the long matches, drawing on the pipe to light it. He poured his tea from the cup into his saucer to cool before supping it, wetting his long whiskers, all the while ignoring Mother's disapproving glances. His working clothes were thick baggy trousers held up by a large leather belt, but his big army-style boots were always well polished. I liked to watch him shave and sharpen his razor on the leather strop before hanging it back on the nail near the kitchen window. Each day he would tend his vegetables, fruit trees, beehives and collect the honey. He grew intensely scented sweet peas beyond the outside toilet and would occasionally drink from a barrel of home-made cider that he kept in the small scullery outside the kitchen. At other times he would sit on his wooden chair at the back door, thoughtfully looking out to the horizon, taking in the beauty of that rolling Dorset countryside with its ancient chalk downs and clifftops. He was a solid citizen of rural England.

Tom lived four years longer than Margaret and ended his days in a nursing home. I visited Granddad Studland once with Father's younger sister Hilda and her husband George. I was sixteen and had just returned from Kenya following Father's death. Granddad appeared content, if more wizened. Much to our amusement, he had acquired a friend who took on the role of a 'lesser rank' to fetch and carry for him. Whatever Tom wanted, his self-appointed batman would scuttle off to get, always eager to please. We left Tom gazing into his distant memories. I may have inherited my love of sitting and thinking from him. It's a pity I've failed to attract a 'lesser rank' to fetch and carry.

I'd like to have known my Studland grandparents when I became an adult. Perhaps I have more in common with Grandma than the fair streak in her hair. I don't know. I loved Granddad for his humour and twinkling blue eyes and today I wonder what stories he might have told me of his time in South Africa and as a London policeman. I have his blue eyes and even temperament. How blessed I feel to know something of my heritage and recognise strands of it in myself.

4 Harmony Terrace, Studland, Dorset

Harmony Terrace in the 1990s

I first met Grandma Studland when I was a baby, but of course my memories of her came from later in my childhood. We stayed with her and Granddad in Studland during the last part of the war until we moved to London. I think Mother found Grandma difficult to get along with at times. Grandma had established routines and Mother was to fit around them as best she could. Mother had her own routines, including taking us for a walk every afternoon, Grandma's black Scottish terrier called Dina trotted behind us. Father was working in London and would come home at weekends, striding across the clifftops from Swanage, where the train line ended. It was a happy day when we were all together again.

Grandma Studland's household routine was typical of the day – church on Sunday, wearing her best but plain hat, followed by washing and bath on Monday, when the fire was lit below the deep copper tub. This was set in a concrete surround fitted into the corner of the kitchen and was the only means of heating sufficient water for the Monday cleaning rituals. Clothes were rubbed on a corrugated washboard, removed with long wooden tongs and squeezed through the mangle's solid rollers. It was heavy, hot work and Grandma would wipe her face with the edge of her floral apron. There were no bathrooms in these old workers' cottages, so the next part of the ritual was to place the tin bath in the centre of the kitchen. One-by-one we had a hot bath, with Granddad the lucky last. No wonder it only happened once a week. Today's daily hot showers are a luxury we ought not to take for granted.

All these activities meant eating cold meat and salad every Monday. Good budgeting brought us shepherd's pie on Tuesdays and other innovative dishes for the rest of the week. Grandma made a mean steam pudding and her baking left me with a lifelong love of fruitcake. The cut-glass biscuit barrel on the sideboard was always full (but limited to us), and we cousins vied to inherit it in later years because of the happy childhood memories it prompted. Cousin Barbara has it.

Grandma may have seemed a dour Scot, but she was kind-hearted. For many years she took care of arthritic Great Aunt Rose, Granddad's widowed sister who came to live with them in Studland. This meant washing and dressing Aunt Rose every morning before bringing her into the sitting room in her wicker wheelchair. I liked Aunt Rose and was rather in awe of her disability and gnarled hands. She would open her little black purse with some difficulty and give Frances and me sixpence for an ice cream.

As a good Scot, Gran's eyes would light up whenever Father arrived with a bottle of a good Scottish whisky. She was a 'just the one' drinker, but she *so* enjoyed it. She also loved a game of whist and would sit at the dining table stroking the protective velvet tablecloth while working on her next move. At 9 o'clock Granddad would wind up the clock on the mantelpiece, the cue to go to bed. In the year before she died, Grandma suffered a form of dementia and some nights she refused to go to bed with Granddad until she had seen their marriage certificate. Her strict standards never slipped, even in her confusion.

We moved to London in 1947 and our visits to Studland continued. Frances and I would sleep in a bedroom above the grocery shop on the opposite side of the road to our grandparents' small cottage. It was the home of kindly shop owners called Mr and Mrs Higginbottom. The shop's distinctive aromas of sliced ham and fresh bread followed us upstairs as we manoeuvred past their large Airedale terrier. The Higginbottom's claim to fame in our small lives was that they were first cousins who had married. We found this particularly intriguing as the thought of marrying any of our many cousins hadn't occurred to us. We thought of them as siblings. Each morning we slid past the over-friendly dog on the polished wooden floors and headed out the back door. Father would guide us safely across the road, back to our grandparents' house, Number 4 Harmony Terrace.

I have rich childhood memories of our Studland holidays. I loved the beaches, cliff-top walks beside meadows edged with ferns and brambles that gave shelter to small creatures. We watched hovering kestrels, swooping sparrowhawks and rabbits being chased down burrows by ferrets. I had a sense of belonging in Studland that I didn't have in Lincoln.

During his retirement, Granddad had a part-time job at the beachside car park where he sat outside a small wooden hut with a ticket machine hung around his shoulders on a leather strap. We thought he was a very important man in his uniform and proudly let friends know he was the 'ticket man'. As a result of this description I was under the illusion for years that the village council chairman ('chair man') collected the money for the deckchairs available for hire on the beach. We'd report to Granddad before walking down to the beach with our buckets and prawning nets. The path was full of pebbles and when it rained it developed deep ruts and a dank pungent smell would rise from the encroaching vegetation watered by ocean-bound streamlets. I once slipped on these pebbles, getting a deep cut on my knee. It was fortunate that we were being followed by our parents on that occasion, as Frances panicked in her concern for me and kept running around a nearby tree. This brought about another family saying; 'Running round a tree' described a time of severe distress.

Frances and I played for hours in the beach's coarse yellow sand and paddled in rock pools, knowing not to climb around the rocks or go into the cliff's caves in case we were cut off by a rising tide. In the frugality of the post-war years we wore home-knitted, mustard-coloured swimming costumes that sagged to our knees as soon as they were wet; an experience that is seared in our memories, and those of our contemporaries.

My sketch of the dreaded orange woollen swimsuits.

Studland was real Enid Blyton country, and like many children of our time, we knew her children's adventure stories well. I read all her books and especially liked the Famous Five and Secret Seven series that were set in Dorset. We played our adventures on the sand dunes and beaches of Studland Bay, sometimes with our cousin Barbara and other children we came to know.

Studland beach was where King George VI, General Montgomery and General Eisenhower observed the troops training for the D-Day landings of April 1944. After the war, the old fortifications around the bay became hiding places for imaginative children. We would hide inside the malodourous bunkers, holding our noses while crouching against green, slimy walls. On the way home to our grandparents we avoided scattered pieces of pipe that were all that remained of Project Fougasse, a defunct experimental defence system involving burning oil on the ocean.

Another favourite place was the graveyard. I liked the crunching sound of our feet on the gravel path that passed the square Norman tower of St Nicholas' Church. A church had been there since AD 940, and Studland's settlement date was AD 250. We were walking on ancestral land and loved to see our family names on the gravestones and invent stories about names on other weather-worn graves. We would read the inscriptions and discuss possible reasons for a child to die so young, or a man to drown at sea. On the way home we chatted about smugglers and pirates.

Studland's coves were used by smugglers for centuries and we always believed that one day we would find a secret passage from the local Manor House Hotel down to the sea. We didn't, but there was something like a dark cobwebbed priest-hole behind a mirror on the hotel's staircase.

My only experience of seeing a ghost was in this cliff-top hotel, but that happened about 50 years later. Frances and I were on a nostalgic visit and had an attic room overlooking the sea. I was sitting on my bed when I saw the figure of a woman dressed in 16th century clothes walk across an alcove towards the window. She stood gazing out to sea, then she was no longer there. I have no explanation for this apparition and it was several days before I told Frances. She was disappointed I hadn't told her earlier.

We took for granted the freedom we had to roam in safety. We watched the cows being milked at the dairy and spent our pocket money on ice cream at the Gould's post office shop. How blessed we were to have experienced this level of peace and safety after our wartime beginnings.

Scattered memories of London

The three years in London are faded images of a semi-detached two-storey house in a North London cul-de-sac with a view of the local gasworks. Over time this area became home to various waves of immigrants. It was a place to try to establish one's family. My mind conjures up the feelings of cold winds and I recall snow-covered low garden walls in the record-breaking winter of 1949. My senses grasp at shadows. There were gaping holes between the rows of shops that told of the war's bomb damage. I have a sense of the smell of caged animals at Whipsnade Zoo and the sawdust at Bertram Mills Circus, where, I was told, the clowns frightened me. There were light summer evenings sleeping to the lullaby of bird calls and waking to the nightmare of catfights. I try to recall Father's voice as he called up the stairs, 'Go to sleep you two!' and we'd giggle before subsiding into sleep. I was four and the memories are muddled with old photographs and family conversations.

The local nursery school enchanted me by being in the attic of a small building next to the primary school. It wasn't called a kindergarten in those post-war years, for obvious reasons. It held a treasure trove of dress-up clothes, games and best of all, little cards of short poems that I took home to learn and recite. I walked home with Frances to be greeted by Mother, a warm fire, hot toast and dripping and the BBC children's hour played on the metal-encased wireless. It was made from an aeroplane wing and later I wondered if it had crashed in the war. Sunday school is remembered mainly for the pretty Bible story stamps that we stuck into a booklet. We were forbidden to play on the street on Sundays, I'm not sure why. Frances would take her little toy oven and tea set into the front garden to play and I would follow her:

'Look at us. We don't care that we can't play in the street today.' Frances pretended and I was content to play with her as the 'lesser rank'. It was a few years before I rebelled about being relegated to 'lesser rank', and much later Frances confessed that this refusal had been a great shock to her.

Audrey, the lesser rank

Other events lodged in my mind for no apparent reason. 'There are bananas at the corner shop,' and we'd rush up to buy some. Rationing was still in place. Clip clop and the rattle of bottles: 'Here comes the milkman.' We'd watch a neighbour dart onto the road to shovel up the horse manure for his garden. 'Poor Mrs Dyke, I'll pop in and see her again later,' Mother said frequently of our neighbour, who had three boys under six. In hindsight years, I suspect she suffered from post-natal depression. Over the road, Wendy was an only child who was made popular by her father's conjuring tricks. 'Can you come to my party?' she asked us when it was her birthday. 'Ooh, please can we go, Mummy?' We took a present, played games and ate jelly and ice cream. I arrived home convinced I could cut a piece of string in two and join it again by chewing the broken ends, as demonstrated by Wendy's father. To my chagrin, it remained in two pieces.

Throughout those years Father was busy establishing the telecommunications system at the new civil airport, Heathrow. It was previously a field next to RAF Heston. I remember we'd call out: 'Here comes Daddy,' as he walked up the garden path, leaving his old Riley car parked by the gate. He arrived home very excited.

'They're going to build a tunnel under the runway and it'll be much quicker getting to work.'

This was the start of years of expansion with roads, underpasses and mushrooming buildings. No more walking across muddy runways to board a flight and no more Nissen huts and tents. In those post-war years, we went to a staff children's Christmas party held in one of the temporary Nissen huts. It was memorable for the sight of Santa arriving from the North Pole in a large aircraft. I was given a doll called Margaret, who opened and shut her eyes. Frances' doll could be fed with a small bottle before wetting its nappy.

Dewdrops from a vanished life that fall lightly into the well of my memory.

The Big Move happened in 1950. Colleagues from Father's war years enticed him to consider working in Kenya, a British Colony in East Africa. He and Mother were already considering a move to either Surrey, Canada or New Zealand, a rather diverse set of options that probably reflected Father's travels. This pending move was of little interest to me until we took the bus to London's West End to buy new clothes. In the autumn we left our school, much to Frances' delight, and travelled into central London. After an overnight stay at the Grosvenor Hotel, the first of many new experiences, we boarded a BOAC Hermes at Heathrow. We were bound for Nairobi.

'Hello, Jimmy. This your family?' The crew were wartime buddies and we were well looked after. We were off to Africa, far from the bomb sites of London. Instead, we flew into the approaching unrest of a colony of Britain's fading Empire.

Reflection

Science tells us the first three years of a child's life are when our neural pathways are established. I'm grateful for the loving pathways that were established in my early years; firm ground for future steps in life.

Two

KENYA CHILDHOOD

Images of Africa flood my mind and fill my heart
with a kind of longing. Yet, when I start
to look beyond this childhood view,
there's beauty here and horror too.
*

Linking lives in bush, coast, plain,
dying in drought, thriving in rain,
dusty roads and rivers of mud,
creatures that crawl and suck your blood.
And yet…
we respond and love the place,
as one small family from a distant race,
accepting its dangers as normal life:
a mellow childhood that closes with strife.

Memories of a childhood spent in Kenya were lodged in the deep recesses of
my mind, and only a few have emerged without wrenching my heart. Some
things have evoked a painful sense of loss, others arrived as flashes of insight
mellowed by the passage of time. The first of these came as the sickly taste
of warm orange juice, drunk at a table in a hall warmed by fetid air being

stirred by large creaking fans. This was the transit lounge at Khartoum. I sat at a table with Mother, staring sleepily at men in long white robes and red hats that to my child's mind looked like flowerpots. We were bound for Nairobi on a BOAC Hermes flight. I remember nothing of the first stop at Rome and the last at Entebbe on the shores of Lake Victoria. The landing in Nairobi became a blur, but I was told we were met by Father's colleagues, who drove us to the guest house on the outskirts of the city centre. The jacaranda-lined avenues of the city created an unforgettable landscape that remained in Mother's memory all of her 99 years.

We stayed at the Thika Road Guest House that hosted all newly arrived government employees and their families. I can still conjure up the smell of the polished wooden floors and red dust, and in my mind's eye, I see the dining room with its white tablecloths and friendly African waiters in their long white kanzus (robes). We were tired from our flight and taken to our rooms along a wide wooden verandah.

'What are those?' I asked, staring at the twisted white nets hanging over our beds. I wondered if they were lampshades.

'Mosquito nets.'

'How do they work?'

'You'll see.'

As we were tucked into bed that night, the room receded behind the swathe of netting that cocooned my bed, bringing me a sense of security beyond the mere exclusion of predatory bugs. The smell of Flit, the common pyrethrum insect repellant, pervaded the room as we slipped into sleep on our first night in East Africa. Little did we know that having been born in one war we were to grow up in one of a different kind. We were distracted by the newness of life around us, getting used to sleeping under nets and living at an altitude of 5800 feet (1795m).

World events were not on our radar, but it was the time when South Africa introduced apartheid, India developed its constitution and the Korean War was beginning. America and Russia began to move into a Cold War, in spite of the 1949 North Atlantic Treaty. Humanity was continuing its merry way into the last half of the twentieth-century bickering, recovering, celebrating, struggling and surviving to populate new generations that always aimed to do better. My family was no different to the many who were trying to improve their lot in life and give the next generation a better deal. We made this move with hope, love and endless curiosity.

Mainly mellow days

It was Sunday afternoon and time to 'go for a run'. Not one that required two-legged effort, but one fuelled by our second-hand Austin A40 car. We were going to the Nairobi National Park to see the animals in their natural but fenced reserve of about 29,000 acres (117.21km²). The Park was established in 1946 through the efforts of conservationist Mervyn Cowie who is the Park's director. We hoped to see lions emerging from their shady daytime hideouts, although several friends said it took more experienced observers than us to spot them.

'Come *on* Audrey!' an irritable voice demanded I get in the car and leave my book behind. I hopped into the back seat with Frances. With no law for seat belts to restrain us, we leaned forward to see where we were going. Father drove up Hurlingham Road where we were now living, cut through to the Ngong Road and headed south on Langata Road. We reached Nairobi West, a small domestic airport later known as Wilson Airport, and Father drew up on the grass verge alongside the perimeter fence. We all had an interest in small planes and stared through the fence as keen 'bird twitchers' of a different kind. The Swahili word for an aeroplane is *ndege* which also means bird. Frances and I often sat in the car outside the control tower at Eastleigh Airport on the other side of Nairobi where Father worked. We were good at identifying types of aircraft and for us it was a form of the game I Spy.

'Which Piper is that?' I asked.

'It's a Cessna, silly!' Frances and I showed off our knowledge of light aircraft and Father joined in.

'See the Tiger Moth? Now that's still a good plane to learn in.'

'Bouncy landing!' I pointed to a plane taking off again.

'He's doing circuits and bumps,' said my informative sister.

In a few years, Frances would learn to fly at Nairobi West Aeroclub with the handsome Sven. At the time she was not sure which she liked the most, flying or Sven. Her dream was to be a commercial pilot, but her poor grounding in mathematics let her down. Although Father always told us girls were just as good as boys, he advised Frances against her chosen career. He'd seen passengers refuse to embark on flights piloted by a woman.

'Come on girls,' Father kept us to time, 'we'll miss the best time for the animals.'

We sat back in our seats as he drove on and we reached the game park entrance around four o'clock. 'Jambo Bwana, *shillingi tina,*' and Father paid the ten-shilling fee for the car, regardless of the number of passengers, and we were given a map.

'*Wapi simba?*' Father managed in his stilted Swahili to ask where we'd find lions. The man pointed to a spot on the park's map and we thanked him, '*Asante*'.

We drew away from the entrance gate, then stopped to check the map. The car following us was bulging with occupants. They'd managed to get their money's worth by cramming in a dozen friends and relatives. We needed to be ahead of their dust on the unsealed road to the 'donga', or valley where we might see some lions. A sign warned us, *Stay in Your Car!* and I added: 'If we get too close, put up your windows or they'll smell us'.

'Oh Audrey, don't be silly, they're not going to eat us,' asserted the equally unsure Frances.

We know about the man-eaters of Tsavo, where an aberrant pair of lions took to killing construction workers along the Tsavo section of the Mombasa to Nairobi railway line. That it happened in 1898 did not detract from the drama nor dampen our keen imaginings.

'Look over there.' Mother pointed to some bushes about 500 yards away. 'See the car near those bushes?' Mother was developing good game-spotting eyes, but this time the clue was the parked car.

'Well spotted,' affirmed Father, and we bumped across the rough grass and down a gradual slope to draw close to the fever trees. If we'd been more alert, we'd have noticed the Thomson's gazelle and zebra were giving the area a wide birth, but we were still novices. Father turned off the ignition and we cruised quietly down the slope until we were about level with the other car, but not too close. The rainy season was over, and the long grass was brown and dry, camouflaging our big cats. We pressed against the car windows peering into the grass, looking for a movement or shape. All was quiet except for the occasional bird call and the buzz of a fly trapped in the car with us. No one spoke until Mother pointed.

'Is that something?' Father picked up the binoculars.

'Yes, I see three of them. I can't see any cubs.'

We took turns to peer through the glasses, and I saw them. Two tawny, rather mangy lionesses were sunning themselves on a patch of crushed grass. Close by sat an impressive, fully-maned lion staring with lazy eyes into the distance. He turned to give us a disinterested glance, then looked away in apparent indifference. His mouth opened in a wide yawn baring large fangs before he lifted his impressive body off the ground. As he did, the black cloud of midges hovering above his back moved with him. He approached one of the females and nudged her from behind placing one enormous paw on her hindquarter, but she turned her head and snarled at him. He moved slightly away with a decidedly disgruntled look. And so, we discovered that some facts of life are more easily learned from lions than the birds and bees. Poor Father, such a reserved man to be faced with the straightforward questioning of his youngest daughter.

We watched for a while and then Father restarted the car. It sputtered and stalled and he tried again; no good. Father took control.

'Keep an eye on the lions!' he said as he opened his door to step outside. 'Hil, release the handbrake now.'

'*Do not get out of the car,*' we quoted in nervous unison from the back seat.

'You just keep your eye on those lions,' Father called back as he pushed the car down the slope with one hand on the steering wheel. The vehicle began to move down towards the lions.

'Get in Daddy!'

'Get in Jim!'

Agreement all round as the car resolutely rolled towards the lions and began to pick up speed. *Where is Father?* He appeared, trotting alongside our back window. Frances began to panic, 'Get in Daddy; get in,' she was near to tears. I was holding my breath. Mother leant over, and reaching down pulled on the handbrake. Father jumped in still puffing, released the brake and pulled the starter. Splutter, the engine fired and Father steered us away. And this was how we were saved from a starring role in an imagined new film called *The Family-Eating Lions of Nairobi*, or so we told our disbelieving friends. Were we in danger? Maybe not, but our ignorance about the animals of our new home was recognised, and that required another book for Father's collection. How he would have loved our modern technology and worldwide web searches.

'Well done, Hil,' he said quietly to Mother.

'Perhaps this is why the Indians have so many in their car,' observed Mother.

'That's a thought; more to push!' agreed Father and his hazel eyes twinkled in amusement. He'd enjoyed himself.

Such a breakdown was never repeated, and we became more familiar with game-spotting. We identified gazelle, zebra, wildebeest, giraffe, ostrich, and birdlife like vultures and elegant secretary birds. Occasionally cheetah and lions were seen, but scary rhinos and elephants were seen mostly on the road to Mombasa, the route to Kenya's coast. We didn't know then that Father would one day be buried in this country he loved, at Langata Cemetery, so close to this place of our Sunday outings.

Less mellow days

'Frances, where's Mummy?' I asked.

'Down the bottom of the plot with Daddy. He's teaching her to shoot.'

'I think I'd like to be able to shoot, but I don't think I could shoot a person.'

'You probably could if they attacked you,' said Frances with unusual pragmatism.

'Maybe.' I paused to consider this and then continued, 'Is Daddy working tonight?'

'Yes, and we'll be in with Mummy again.'

'I'm sleeping in the orange chairs.'

'You did last time. It's my turn.' Frances pouted and we waited for Mother's arbitration of our sisterly squabble. That night I smiled as I snuggled into my bed of two well-cushioned armchairs pushed together near the window. Sometimes it was good to be the youngest, and shorter.

The shooting practice was one outcome of Kenya's Emergency, a war of a different kind that had crept up on us. The colony had become less secure due to the Kenyans' push for independent rule. Britain opposed this saying the Colony was not ready, and the resultant unrest raised up a movement of guerrilla fighters known as the Mau Mau. Its members infiltrated the dominating Kikuyu tribe and over time the fighting extended to a form of civil war with the larger tribes competing for supremacy in anticipation of independent rule.

We liked and trusted the Kikuyu people who worked for us in our rented city home and garden. Yet, there were too many stories of the Mau Mau forcing their tribal brothers to take strong oaths that bound them to kill their white employers. Our parents decided to move to a safer area away from the city centre and Kikuyu lands. I was sorry to lose the gardener who rescued me when I became stuck high in the large pine tree in the front garden. I missed Wainena's steam puddings and the fresh-picked mealies (corn cobs) cooked on his charcoal fire. My grasp of Swahili language faltered through reduced opportunities for conversation. Frances and I had already moved schools three times, and our move out of town meant yet another change of school.

We moved to an area about forty minutes' drive south of the city, beyond the Langata entrance to the national game park. First, we lived in a rental house built by someone known as 'Old Mad Bailey'. I was never given a satisfactory explanation for his nickname, except that his houses were built using trial and error. A large, square, grey-stone pillar in the centre of our lounge room corrected the error of a sagging roof in our new home. We announced our arrival in the neighbourhood by erecting our name board at the beginning of our driveway. 'J.S.W. Payne' in plain black script on the white wooden board told something of its namesake's lack of pretension. All houses were marked by their occupant's name. There were no street numbers and mail was collected from boxes at the local post office.

Christmas day at Langata house

Our house stood back from a quiet road with a view across a deep valley to wide plains edged by the distant undulations of the Ngong Hills. Sitting on our verandah, we would watch small groups of giraffe cross the plain with their rocking strides. At nightfall, we'd see the glow of low grass fires that chased frightened animals. In the rainy season, we'd listen to the amorous frogs singing to their sweethearts under the dripping undergrowth. Standing on the hillock that was our hedged vegetable garden, we'd count the gaps between lightning and thunder.

There were times when Father used his flashlight to converse in Morse code with the brother of our school friend who lived a few miles away. A telephone might have been easier, but Morse code was more fun for a young boy and a young-at-heart radio operator.

'Can Audrey and Frances come to play with Lesley tomorrow?' de-dot-de-da would flash across the darkened night sky.

'Yes. Will come at nine.' Father came indoors looking very pleased with himself.

Our journeys to school became more exciting during the rains as Father had to negotiate a few boggy patches and avoid deep ditches. We'd hang on tight at a particularly boggy section of road that passed by Karen Blixen's old farm and house. She was the famous Danish pioneer of the area, Baroness Karen von Blixen-Finecke. She wrote Danish fables under the name of Isak Dineson, and her Kenya autobiography, *Out of Africa*, begins with the words, '*I once had a farm in Africa…*'. Years later a friend of mine, Errol Trzebinski, published the story of Karen Blixen's romance with Denys Finch-Hatton, an English big-game hunter. Errol's book was combined with Blixen's book to create the 1985 film *Out of Africa*. I first heard of Karen Blixen when I went with Father to buy chicken coops from her farm.

The chicken coops were needed after we moved out of the rental house into our own house a few miles away. That house was built by Father, a more careful builder than Old Mad Bailey. His eagle eye watched every stage and he did much of the work himself. I helped by holding pipes and watching electrical wiring being put in place. Later we would discuss the placement of a pond, trees and shrubs, and I'd listen to his ideas, adding my own.

Our nameboard went up, but I was more impressed with our neighbour's nameboard. Instead of stating Ivan Hook it displayed pictures of an eye, a van and a hook. I admired this innovation and wished our name would lend itself to something similar. The next project was the erection of a large deep-litter chicken house and Father was once again about to make a mythical fortune. I learned about Rhode Island Reds and Leghorns and helped collect eggs, until the hens became infested with red mite and I began to itch. Before this chicken fortune could be made, we moved again because our parents set their sights on the purchase of a coastal smallholding and early retirement.

Meanwhile, we were embroiled in civil defence precautions and Mother was learning to shoot in a clearing just beyond the henhouse, at the bottom of our five-acre block. Frances and I quietly honed our skills with a catapult.

⁓

The picture is clear in my mind. We were sleeping in our parent's bedroom, and I was once again snuggled down in the armchairs. All girls together with Father away on his night shift at Eastleigh Airport. I noted he always took a pillow, perhaps to sleep in a chair if they weren't busy. Mother was awake most of the night, and the gun slept under her pillow. Frances took up Father's side of the double bed and slept fitfully. As the youngest, I had infinite faith in the protection of my Mother and Sister. I slept like a log, as did Pincher our large dog, who was ensconced in his basket at the other end of the house. In the morning we noticed paw marks in the garden bed below the bedroom window. Lions came by, or maybe it was a leopard looking for a tasty dog. No wonder Pincher kept quiet. He was an intelligent dog; a Doberman Pinscher crossed with an Alsatian. After breakfast, I continued my 'training' of him.

'Sit,' and he sat.

Then I wore dental braces and my 's' became 'sh'. The family encouraged me to repeat the same command with my new speech defect, and I innocently obliged by saying 'Shit' and blushing in embarrassment. Koko, our parrot, quickly learnt this new pronunciation of 'sit!' which extended the amusement and further confused Pincher, who fortunately did not obey this unique command.

Koko was good company and a clear talker like all African Greys. He or she (we never knew which) was unable to fly because one wing was damaged when she was captured as a chick in West Africa. She loved Father, hated all women and had a vicious beak. But because she chose to call out apt phrases at the right time, she kept us very amused. The handiest one was that she repeatedly said goodbye in a forceful voice when visitors lingered too long by the front door. At night her cage was covered with a green cloth which she habitually chewed to make a peephole.

'Helloo-oo!' said the tentative voice attached to the beady eye peeping through the hole. We were glad of the distraction Koko brought us on the nights Father was away.

The Mau Mau Uprising was a way of life that became the new norm for us. It was a brutal time and we all lived cautious lives. Our exposure to these brutalities was minimal, unlike some of the up-country settler families and a more significant number of Kenyans, who suffered at the hands of both Mau Mau and the government forces. We'd heard of murdered settlers in the highlands and other atrocities closer to home. We grew accustomed to seeing European men going about their daily lives wearing holstered guns. Frances and I waved at the soldiers in the passing army trucks and looked to the skies as another Lincoln bomber flew overhead to drop its load on terrorist gangs hiding in the Aberdare Forest.

One morning we arrived at our school, Woodley Primary, to hear that the night watchman had been found bleeding and near death outside the school's office.

'We pray this morning for John,' said Headmaster Wilson at morning assembly. We all bowed out heads and many prayed earnestly, but we heard nothing more about him.

During school holidays we spent our days at Maryland Riding School. During a hack we rode past a village where a man threw an iron stake towards my horse. As the horse shied, I fell off. I was unhurt but felt shocked by both the action of the man and the horse. I enjoyed horse riding until that time at Maryland's but after that event I lost interest.

The half-hour drive home from the stables took us along the Langata Road. Just before the Banda turn-off, the road dipped into a deep forested valley with a particularly steep descent. Frances and I enjoyed sitting on the floor of the car for this section of our journey. We'd discovered the thrill of the G-force when the car hit the bottom of the valley and accelerated upwards. We were still sitting on the floor one early evening when Father barked, 'Stay on the floor!' Naturally, we immediately wanted to see what was happening.

'Stay down!' His voice was urgent and commanding.

We cowered in the well of the car and Mother was bent double in the front passenger seat. Father sped away to the sound of receding gunfire. Frances and I peeped out of the rear window to see men with raised guns running across the road into the opposite bush. We looked at one another with wide eyes, bombarded our parents with questions while it slowly sank in just how close terrorist action had come. Reality hit home and we stopped complaining about the restrictions that were placed on some of our activities.

Overall our level of risk remained lower than many others, and it wasn't until years later when I had a conversation with a Kikuyu nursing colleague that I gained more perspective. Her brother disappeared forever, and her childhood was far more troubled than mine. Even so, it was not easy to read of Mau Mau veterans being hailed as heroes in later years. The Kenya Emergency officially ended in 1960, the year after I left school. It was a war of a different kind.

A Mix Of Mellow Memories

It was against this backdrop of unrest and insecurity that our childhood days continued. Frances chose to go to ballet classes, where I eventually joined her. Madam Zerkovich was delighted with Frances' talent and less impressed with mine.

'Good Frances…Audrey, point zee toe,' she urged, as pained exasperation passed over her face.

My early love of fairies that had caused me to haunt the library for fairy stories, did not translate into my dancing like one, nor was it helped by my habit of extruding my tongue in concentration. However, in the ballet school's end-of-year stage performance, I could be identified in a photograph as the only chorus girl smiling as we danced the can-can.

Primary School years

In 1953, there was an air of excitement at school followed by a distribution of small Union Jacks on sticks. Princess Elizabeth and Prince Philip were to visit Kenya and we were to wave our flags as they arrived at Eastleigh Airport. This we dutifully did. The royal couple toured Nairobi National Park, where their car did not break down like ours had done two years before. They were driven up country to Nyeri and were at Tree Tops Lodge when the news broke that King George VI had died and their young married lives changed forever.

'Why are you crying?' I asked Frances after we heard the news.

'The King is dead.' I was puzzled by her emotion and thought she was overreacting.

'But we didn't *know* him.' My young logic did nothing to defuse her rising emotion.

'Oh, *Audrey.*' She disappeared to grieve in private. How I must have irritated her.

Our year group of children, born during World War II, was small, and new schools were built to accommodate the significant increase of post-war Baby Boomers that followed. We were re-zoned to these new schools according to where we lived, and we were moved several times. By the time we reached our last year of primary school we were at Woodley Primary and there were seven children in my class. Along with my peers, my life has been marked by this following generation. Our generation has pushed boundaries, but it has been the Baby Boomers who had the numbers to create change. Sometimes I feel like saying, 'We thought of it first!' But maybe it's all in my mind as I can't think of a concrete example.

Home Leave

Our schooling was interrupted twice to go on home leave to England. Home leave was a better version of the Australian long service leave because it required overseas employees to return to England for three months every three years, on full pay. There were variations of this arrangement but this is how it worked for Father. Our return fares had some limitations on the class of travel, which was determined by an employee's pay grade. We sailed with Union Castle Line and had second-class cabins. We had fun at the Crossing of the Line (Equator) Ceremony, took part in fancy dress parties and played deck games. Mostly we spent hours swimming in a canvas swimming pool. This was slung over an opening in the deck. I occasionally wondered where we might end up if the canvas tore.

At times Father would call us to see points of interest.

'Look over here, girls!' At the ship's railing we'd see a whale, then watch the glistening flying fish skim over the water beside the ship.

'Why do they fly?' we asked.

'Maybe bigger fish are chasing them.' I dreamt of the ship sinking and these bigger fish. This would have meant using our childish 'shark defence', which was to sing God Save the Queen under water. Frances and I used to practise this in the bath when we were younger. I never got beyond the first line. Mother had no such worries and enjoyed the relaxation and new experiences of these cruises.

Our first trip took us through the Suez Canal, stopping in Port Said. There, a rush of small boats known as bum boats anchored alongside. Swarthy men called out their wares and waved ivory fans, silver and gold necklaces and leather goods. A man came on board to entertain us with fluffy baby chicks and conjuring tricks. Other passengers haggled and threw coins over the side of the ship for young boys to dive and retrieve from the murky depths of the harbour. I felt sorry for the children and was uncomfortable with the offhand way some of the passengers treated the Egyptians, who seemed very poor. Father was familiar with all this from his seafaring days and enjoyed explaining the scenes around us.

I spotted a large statue of a horse and rider and wondered about it. It was the memorial for the Desert Mounted Corps who fought in World War I. Erected in 1932, it commemorated the bravery of the soldiers and their mounts from England, Australia and New Zealand. This snippet of information lay fallow until our next trip through the Suez Canal in 1957. Meanwhile, we went ashore to buy gifts for our many relatives. On our return journey from England, we purchased a camel stool that was a type of a saddle. It remains in the family.

Our second sea voyage to England was in 1957 when the Second Arab-Israeli War and the Suez Crisis had just ended. Egypt's President Gamal Nasser had nationalised the canal and Britain, France and Israel tried to regain control of it. America, Russia and the United Nations applied political pressure to get a withdrawal. I had little understanding of this, only noticing the army trucks and lack of friendliness on our second journey.

'Where's that big statue we saw last time, Daddy?'

'I heard it was smashed by the Egyptians.'

I discovered in later years that a duplicate of the statue was recast in the early 1960s and by 1964 the memorial, complete with the original base of granite blocks with bullet holes, was unveiled on top of Mt Clarence in Albany, Western Australia. There it's known as the ANZAC Desert Mounted Corps Memorial and commemorates the Light Horse Brigade as well as the New Zealand Mounted Rifles, the Imperial Camel Corps and the Australian Flying Corps. They served in Egypt, Palestine and Syria between 1916 and 1918. Albany was the last sight of land for the majority of the Australian and New Zealand troops as their ships sailed away to fight in World War I. That war decimated a generation of Australian young men who died needlessly on the Turkish lines at Gallipoli, in the French trenches and elsewhere. When I first arrived in Albany in 1972, I recognised the memorial and a flutter of amazement and nostalgia ran through me.

On those childhood UK holidays, we lived out of our suitcases and tried not to interrupt our many relatives' usual routines, and watched their favourite TV programmes. We enjoyed having time with our many cousins and tried to get out of doing our allocated school work. Our family was always glad to be home again in Kenya, even if it meant moving into yet another house, and doing more cleaning.

High School years

My last school years were spent as a boarder at the Kenya High School for Girls (KHS), where I had four happy years of good teaching and good friendships. There was homesickness at the start of each term, along with aching muscles as I accustomed my legs to the school's many steps and daily sports activities. My sporting ability was hampered by undiagnosed childhood asthma and I fainted easily after exertion. Team leaders rarely chose me for their teams, but my good friend Sheelagh rescued me by training me for hockey with her usual relentless determination. I became the proud and bruised goalkeeper for our Hamilton House hockey team. Sadly, Sheelagh's persistence failed in the swimming pool and I remained the only girl in my year to achieve no more than a red swimming cap, denoting my ability to swim but inability to dive off the second diving board. This particular inability had nothing to do with my tendency to faint, although it might have been a useful way to force a dive. I simply hated the thought of falling from any height headfirst.

Gill, Kathleen (Kaye), Sheelagh and me outside our boarding house.

The Kenya High School headmistress was Miss Stott whose initials JAM give her the nickname of Jami. She was a devout Christian and the aunt of John Stott, a theologian and evangelist of renown. This caused her to approve of the school's several Bible fellowship groups that were initiated by Christian teachers and students. One of these teachers also taught me Latin, and when I complained that it was a dead language and no one could speak it, she taught us to sing 'Three Blind Mice' in Latin. I was impressed, but more amused by the effect her writing on the blackboard had on the design of her skirt. The skirt's horizontal line of ships would appear to bounce along waves as her hips moved in response to her writing. But I liked her and went along to the fellowship groups.

I think I 'gave my life to the Lord' several times without really understanding what I was doing, and so this step of faith was put on pause for the next twenty-five years. I was confirmed with my peers at Nairobi Anglican Cathedral and remember the disappointment I felt when nothing mysterious happened as the bishop laid hands on my head.

Over the years, I have kept in touch with a handful of friends from these high school years, although our lives have continued along divergent paths and countries. When we meet, we reminisce over some things and are relieved some things are lost within the passages of time.

Midnight feasts were things I disliked intensely and even the food didn't make them enjoyable. I preferred my sleep. Dances at the Prince of Wales boys' high school (nicknamed the Cabbage Patch) were a highlight of our last year of school. All I recall is being pressed against a tall boy's shirt buttons during a dance and being worried no one else would ask me to dance. We recalled fire alarms, our house matrons, school plays and choirs. 'Ha! Ha!' we'd all laugh at memories mellowed with hindsight.

⌒

Our house in Langata had been sold to pay for ten acres close to Mombasa. Although the Mombasa property pleased me, this meant returning to live in Nairobi in a new apartment, on the third floor. Around this time, boys became more important and Frances and I befriended two neighbours, the

Deas-Dawlish brothers who were about our age. We spent most of the holidays in their company and Sheelagh joined us at times. In time, she was kissed by Hugh and I had my first date with a South African neighbour called Jimmy. His home smelt of polish and every piece of furniture shone in the gloom of lace-curtained windows. Jimmy's hair was dark and sleek against his head and he was the perfect gentleman when we went to the pictures together. We held hands and I admired him for sticking to the courage of his convictions by not standing for the British National anthem. I was also somewhat horrified that he did this, but refrained from telling him so, or that my grandfather fought in the Boer War.

As typical teenagers of our era, we spent our Saturday mornings loitering in the listening booths of Nairobi's record shops. We played the latest hits of the changing music scene of the 1950s like Bobby Darin, Paul Anka and Neil Sedaka. Elvis Presley films were banned by the government which feared a teenage riot. We bought samosas in the Indian bazaar and at the end of the morning Frances and I would meet our parents in Torrs Hotel or the New Stanley.

I continued to be an avid reader, devouring books written by Zane Grey, Georgette Heyer and Elizabeth Gouge. There was no television and our treat was to go to the special films screened for children on some Saturday mornings. We cheered the cowboys and booed any villains. Girls were upstairs and boys downstairs, which left the girls vulnerable to some of the predatory male ushers, who came in once the auditorium was dark. We mostly acquired 'brothers' who were allowed to sit with us.

Meanwhile, politicians were discussing Kenya's move towards independence and the Mau Mau Uprising had officially ended. Kenya was my home country. Father and Mother were looking forward to early retirement and moving to our Mombasa smallholding, where Father would make yet another mythical fortune by growing fruit and hydroponic vegetables. I was hoping to go into Sixth Form and begin a career path, although I was undecided about what this might be. Frances was attending secretarial college in Nairobi and had a growing social life. KoKo, the parrot, was pronouncing 'good morning' in a muffled voice that we discovered was Father's early morning greeting without his false teeth. Mother was cooking roast chicken and giving us sherry trifle as a treat, and we tackled the Sunday cryptic cross-word together as a family, admiring Mother's ability to solve elusive answers. Then the bigger change began.

I was at school one Sunday afternoon, sitting in the back of the family car, which by then was a Morris Isis to suit our impending move to the coast. I was munching on homemade scones when the next life change was announced.

'We have something to tell you,' said Mother, bending round from her front seat. The look on her face put me on alert immediately; something was up.

'Daddy and I need to go to England.'

'I need to have an operation on my lungs,' Father explained in a matter of fact tone, and as I let this sink in, he continued. 'I tripped down some stairs at work and coughed up a bit of blood. They sent me for X-rays, and tests show some spots in my lungs that are cancer.'

I tried to absorb what he was saying as Mother continued. 'The chest hospital is in London and so I'm going too. I'll stay with Aunty Gertrude and Uncle Tom.'

Later, Father regaled me with details of how they could shoot gold seeds around a tumour to contain its growth. I found this very interesting, and it took my mind off the seriousness of the situation. But in the car I was still gathering my thoughts. Then I began to ask questions with childish self-focus. When would they go and, 'What about Frances and me?'

I expected Father to have treatment, then come home cured. This ignorance changed as their time away extended to six months.

Frances stayed with a childless couple who were our parent's friends, and I lived with Sheelagh's family at Mwitu, their home in an area called Karen about half an hour's drive out of the city. I was treated with great kindness and generosity by her parents Frank and Doreen. It was there that I learnt more social skills although I remained very shy in adult company.

We holidayed in places I'd not seen and spent a short time upcountry on the Williams' Kinangop farm. They were school friends of Sheelagh, but they tolerated my tagging along. The last term at the high school approached and Sheelagh and I studied together for our Cambridge Overseas School Certificate exams. A list of French phrases was stuck on the wall beside the toilet for our memorising. It was obvious where people had been when they returned saying things like '*au secours!*' (help!) or '*ouvrez la fenêtre*' (open the window). I persevered with the Latin revision of Caesar's *Gallic Wars*, which I found endlessly boring, and Virgil, who I enjoyed. Sheelagh's photographic memory stood us both in good stead for history revision. These and other mellow memories of a Kenya childhood and holidays with Sheelagh and her parents were a comfort to me as a significant life transition approached.

Reflection

Do not boast about tomorrow, for no one knows what the day may bring.
Proverbs 27:1

Worrying about what the future holds can only spoil the enjoyment of the present. These childhood days seemed ordinary at the time; I knew no different. I felt safe because I had my family around me and I was a compliant child. Hindsight has reinforced how fortunate I was to have these childhood experiences, and to have been 'hedged about' by good friends and traditional family values. I'm uncomfortable as I look back at Britain's well-meaning paternalism and my position of privilege in one of their colonies. I'm also proud of the good that was done. I find no reason to be defensive about the things I grew up to consider normal. But we all need to keep an open mind and be prepared to change our opinions. Life changes and it can change us.

Three

The Big Transition

You may need to have tissues handy for this chapter.

They buried my father
I did not go;
and so...
I buried the grief.
*

I return years later
More aware
and then...
Grief unearthed.
*

Exhumed anger
Late and long.
I know...
They buried my father
And I should have gone.

It was a purple morning in November 1959. Purple avenues lined with the slender limbs and purple-blue panicles of jacaranda trees in bloom. Purple because of the looming cloud of a much loved and respected man coming home to die. We watched as a wizened old man was wheeled across the tarmac of Nairobi's new Embakasi Airport. He clutched the arms of the wheelchair as it bumped along towards the arrivals hall, as I clutched the hand of my guardian.

'Uncle Frank is that Daddy?'

How can he be that man, so gaunt and weak? But yes, it was my Daddy, and the thinner, tired looking woman with him was my Mother. I was 16 years old and felt like reverting to my early childhood as I realised everything was changing significantly, and life was not going to return to normal. I had felt secure with Frank and Doreen and my best friend Sheelagh for the last six months. I'd been treated like another daughter and begun to come out of my shyness. Now I was back to the reality of my sick Father returning from London after treatment for lung cancer. He had lived a full 52 years, and my Mother was soon to be a widow at forty-five.

During those first few months of his return home, I helped Father wash and shave each morning while Mother drove Frances to work. We talked about his time at the Brompton Chest Hospital in London.

'Do you know,' he said, 'there were people from all walks of life in there, and no one knows why we all got cancer.'

'Look, I'm putting on weight,' he enthused standing on the scales in the corner of his bedroom. We were blind to the excess fluid and his worsening condition.

One evening a colleague visited him. Later Father told how he surprised himself by blurting out to this friend, 'I've been waiting for you.' The colleague, an earnest Christian, led him through the Lord's Prayer and Father wept. Maybe Mother told us this later. She said Father felt guilty about waiting so late in life to return to God. Like the biblical parable of the prodigal son, he returned to a loving Father in his desperation. I realised much later that Father had returned to the quiet, trusting faith of his childhood, absorbed as a boy soprano in a church choir. After a lifetime of travel, he placed his end-of-life journey into God's hands. His life had been guided by

Christian ethics, so perhaps it was the war or his enforced childhood church attendance that kept him from later participation. As a family, we rarely went to church.

Mother coped well during these last months of Father's life, putting on a brave face for our sake. It was a sad time. We tried to maintain a lightness in our chatter and included him in all we were doing. He sat in his armchair less often and eventually remained in bed. A nurse and some friends visited, but others couldn't bear to see him fading away. He found that hurtful but understood. Many of his peers had seen too much death during World War II. Reality began to set in for me when Mother said, with tears in her eyes, 'I don't even have a black dress.' The three of us went to buy one.

In January 1960 Father was admitted to Nairobi Hospital and asked that Frances and I not see him in his present physical distress. He didn't want this to be our last memory of him, but 45 years later Frances and I have a conversation.

'Do you wish you'd seen Daddy in hospital?' Frances asked me.

'Not really, although I would like to have said a proper goodbye.'

'I always thought he was writhing around in agony.'

I was upset that she had carried this image all these years. 'I'm sure they would have given him pain relief like morphia, and Mother said he was in an oxygen tent. I don't believe he would have suffered like you imagine.'

I had no way of being sure of this, but I knew my Sister's fertile imagination. It was good to put some of her imaginings to rest, especially as she was undergoing chemotherapy when she asked the question.

I was lying in bed at ten o'clock on the evening on the 31st of January 1960 when the phone rang. Father had died. I'd just finished telling God that I knew my Daddy was dying and would he please take him out of his pain. I'd just let him go.

On the day of the funeral, I was given the option not to attend, which I took because I was in an emotional whirl and didn't want to grieve in public. Father's legacy of reserve and British stiff upper lip lay heavily on me and came back to bite me over the next two decades of unresolved grief. The many facets of loss caused by Father's death included the loss of a stable home, loss of family life, loss of country and the end of school routines and friends. My life swung into free fall, and I entered a time of enormous transition.

⟶

Mother and I went to the evening service at Nairobi's Anglican Cathedral on the following Sunday, and the evangelical preacher closed with an altar call. Mother left her seat and walked to the front. *What is she doing?* I found myself following her. Up I walked to join the six or seven people who were standing for all to see, but with their backs to the congregation. I was shy, fearful and already regretting my decision. Someone prayed for us and I was taken aside by a pretty young woman who invited me to the youth group that Wednesday. I enjoyed this group and its activities. Little did I realise, but this was another step in my long journey to a full profession of belief in Christ. The groundwork had been laid in my Scottish baptism, early Sunday School lessons in London and high-school influences in Kenya. The seed had been planted and lay dormant. Mother remained with her renewed faith until she died, aged ninety-nine. During all this Frances was coping outwardly with her usual bravado, but all was not well with any of us. Grief made its home in the depths of our hearts and minds.

As a family, we decided that our best option was to return to England, where a large extended family could provide initial support. Kenya was moving restlessly towards an independent government and unknown future. Goodbyes were hard; I was withdrawn and not my usual self. Our good humour was lodged in our throats as we set sail on the Donattar Castle from Mombasa. It was a familiar journey up the east coast of Africa, through the Suez Canal, the Mediterranean and across the Bay of Biscay into the English Channel. We each silently recalled the last time we came this way with Daddy in charge, explaining the nuances of ocean voyages and life in the ports we visited. Everything reminded us of him.

Return to England,
England...foreign to me.
Family...gallons of tea.
Confusion...who are we?

The murky waters of the Thames slipped by as we progressed upstream towards Tilbury Docks. We passed rows of identical houses with their jumble of backyards and lines of washing. How small and grubby everything seemed, even in spring. The horizon closed in on the enormity of my loss, squeezing my heart into a painful ball. These last few miles felt more like a journey into a new sort of wilderness than coming home.

Whose home is this? Not mine anymore; the wide-open spaces of Africa are my home.

At sixteen I moved into a life that was simultaneously expanding and contracting. My soul was doing the same, groaning as it fought off the darkness hammering at its door. Waves of unacknowledged anger lapped at my feet.

How could he do this to us? How dare he die and leave us alone! How will Mother and Frances cope without his steadying influence? How will I?

I held onto Father's mantra of 'This too will pass'. As it turned out, it did not pass and none of us did very well in those transitional years.

This Big Transition was not the flowering of mine or Frances' youth as the ensuing few years dragged us from naivety to the brutal reality of life in adulthood. We coped as best we could within the limitations of our life experience. I became concerned that life was short and I need to get on with it, much to the amusement of my Aunt Gladys when I share this insight with her. I found England's regional accents and underlying class system confusing and began to question where I'd fit in this formally delineated way of life. Normal teenage self-questioning like 'Who am I?' bubbled to the surface only to be submerged by yet another wave of life events.

A Notable Event

Mother remarried within a year of Father's death. Pop, as we learned to call him, had employed Mother as his housekeeper. She took this work to provide us with a home in the spacious flat that was attached to his large Lincolnshire farmhouse, outside Boston. Pop had been married twice and both wives had died. He wined and dined Mother and asked her to marry him. She told me later that she thought she could give us and his two teen-age sons some stability. A third, older son had already married and farmed nearby. Mother wanted security and purpose in life and she was a woman used to a patriarchal world and having a man around. Pop pushed the marriage forward and they married by special licence at a church in Westminster, London.

'I knew I'd made a mistake the first night we were married,' Mother confessed to me in later years. We never moved into the flat.

Mother would not break her marriage vows throughout the seven years that Pop broke his to her by drinking his way out of repeated episodes of depression. He abused mother verbally, emotionally and then physically behind closed doors. If I was present and answered back or openly protected Mother, Pop would take this out on her later. I learned great self-discipline. When I was away, I lived in dread of a phone call informing me of an assault. I came home for Christmas most years, which was the season of increased alcoholic spirits for Pop and not much joy for the family. On the Christmas week that I now recount, Pop was at the pub and Mother decided to decamp to my bedroom before he came home. He drank brandy at Christmas which increased his propensity for anger and violence. This memory is clear, even now.

We heard the front door slam shut, a sound that haunted me for many years. It was not a good sign.

'Hilda!' the handle of our locked bedroom door rattled.

'Don't go Mummy.' We sat in silence.

The hammering on the bedroom door persisted for what seemed an eternity, and the voice roared at us. All went quiet, then Pop returned, again and again. We sat on the far side of the room quiet as mice, and tremors ran through me. I'd never felt so vulnerable and powerless.

'I'd better go.' Mother gave in for my sake. In a moment of quiet, she opened the door, walked down the corridor, turned left, then right and entered their bedroom. I sat motionless on my bed with my ears straining for the slightest sound. *Where are the boys when I need them?* I liked my stepbrothers, who proved their worth in later years by continuing to provide for Mother, according to Pop's final wishes. Suddenly my bedroom door burst open and a large object was flung into the room.

'You'd better have this now.' Pop spat out the words from the corridor.

The flying object was my Christmas present, a beautiful sheepskin jacket. At first, I thought I'd return it, but I'm easily dissuaded by Mother. Perhaps this was his way of apologising, but it felt like an insult.

'You see, he's not all bad,' said Mother. How often do we hear that sentiment repeated by victims of abuse?

Mostly these abuses happened when my stepbrothers were out. Whenever they were aware of what was happening, they would handle the situation. On occasions, Pop would be committed under mental health provisions and admitted to a local clinic for treatment. Police would adhere to the unspoken rule of not interfering in cases of domestic violence. Later when Frances was married and living in Norfolk, Mother would drive to her and stay until Pop 'dried out' or settled down. He was always repentant and promised to reform. Mother felt ashamed of her situation and only let her favourite sister, Eileen, know what happened. We all learned to keep quiet about it because of the social stigma.

I decided years later that Pop was an unhappy man with traits of kindness that became submerged in alcoholism and behaviours linked with undiagnosed bipolar depression. His spoilt childhood did him what my mother called, 'a power of no good'. However, Pop's modern farming practices gained him respect and a good income. I enjoyed the creature comforts of his home, and he could be very generous if he liked you.

The smart sheepskin jacket lasted me about twenty years. It also cushioned me when I crashed my first car, a Volkswagen Beetle into the wall of Headington Hill in Oxford. The car had backfired, causing me to take my eyes off the road, and I veered into the hillside's retaining wall. I spent several days in bed with minor concussion and learned to keep my eyes on the road.

Pop died suddenly of an unrelated illness (acute pericarditis) seven years after his marriage to Mother. His eventual bequest gave Mother a house and financial security for her lifetime. My stepbrothers honoured their father's wishes and were very kind to Mother throughout her long life. Their generosity gave me the freedom to lead my own life. Every cloud has a silver lining. Or as my high school mathematics teacher, Mrs McFie would quote: Sufficient unto the day is the evil thereof. (Matthew 6:34). Not that I understood or heeded its meaning. I continued to worry about what might happen next.

Another Notable Event

This was the unexpected birth of a much-loved niece in 1961. The news broke when Mother, Frances and I were sitting on our beds in a hotel room in St Albans. I had an interview at Oaklands Horticultural College the next day. Frances and I were in our pyjamas, and I was sitting on my bed facing her and Mother. The details remain with you at these times.

'We have something to tell you,' Mother started.

I was on red alert. *Is she leaving Pop? No, the tone is wrong*, and my analytical mind went into overdrive.

I looked at Frances, 'You're pregnant?'

'How do you know that?' she stared in amazement.

'I don't know. It just came to me.'

I had no idea how this came to me, maybe it was a nuance of Frances' body language. The story unfolded over the next few days and months.

Frances was never short of male admirers, and she dearly wanted a home and family of her own. She missed our father and his stabilising influence. When she became pregnant to an agricultural student from Cirencester College, she expected the young man to marry her, but he would not. His parents were devastated by their son's behaviour and his mother Pippa remained friends with Frances and they kept in touch until Pippa died.

A child outside of marriage was a social stigma in the 1960s. Pop threw Frances out of his home calling her a slut, which she wasn't. She spent her pregnancy in a small guesthouse in Forest Row near East Grinstead, close to the boy's parents, giving a story to the other residents that her husband was overseas. I don't think they believed her, but they accepted her story at face value. She spent her final weeks of pregnancy at an Anglican home for unmarried mothers close to London.

It was a difficult labour in a hospital where unmarried mothers were treated with a peculiar lack of empathy. I trained as a midwife in later years and what Frances told me of her treatment by the midwives horrified me. Their attitude was punitive – 'You got yourself into this, my girl. Get on with it.'

These often-naive young women were left to labour alone and with minimum pain relief. It broke my heart when Frances eventually disclosed this to me, but none of it quashed the love she had for her baby. I visited her several times in the guesthouse and the home. The arrival of Little Audrey, her temporary name, was a joy to us both. Frances doted on her daughter in the ten weeks she was required to nurse her until the adoption. I loved to hold Little A and the loss of her left a significant gap in our family. I will never know how Frances came to terms with losing her, even though she was assured that her daughter had gone to a good home in Scotland.

Some forty years later, after years of fruitless searching and blocked access to records, Little A was traced by a social worker who had a heart for relinquishing mothers. By that time I was aware of Britain's child migrant scheme, and when I learned that this policy was still in place in the early 1960s, I became very concerned that Little A might have been sent overseas. Frances had seen a television program about the social worker's tireless advocacy for mothers and contacted her. The social worker agreed to help, even waiving part of the usual fee. After some difficulty, she traced Little A to a couple in Scotland, who had named her Theresa. Frances had always liked the name Fenella, and I expect Theresa would be pleased to know she didn't get that name. She'd been given a good home and education and was a cordon bleu cook. I like to think that these are her great-grandmother, Margaret Payne's, genes emerging. Theresa worked as a nanny/housekeeper to an American family living in Bermuda. She was found when Frances was in hospital recovering from a mastectomy for breast cancer. I met Theresa thirteen years later, during the final hours of Frances' life. Today it's a joy to be able to tell people I have three nieces.

This 21ˢᵗ Century Christian chorus by Matt Redman is one that brings tears each time I sing it:

> *God, you give and take away,*
> *Oh, you give and take away.*
> *Yet my heart will choose to say*
> *Lord, blessed be Your name.²*

Losses combined and handed over to God, yet again. I wish I'd known in those teenage years that I would emerge from this Big Transition as a stronger, independent woman. People go through worse, and I'm grateful for the limitations of my experiences. My life journey proceeded down a different road to those of Frances and Mother.

Reflection

'Sufficient unto the day is the evil thereof.' (Matthew 6:34). Writing about these things has been emotional, stretching old scars and opening old wounds that have festered for years. It's been a cleansing process. Jesus said, 'Anyone who starts to plough and then keeps looking back is of no use for the Kingdom of God.' (Luke 9:62). Maybe, but I've almost finished my life's ploughing, and by looking back I see how the distance of years has given me better perspective. My worrying did not change anything, and resentment is best replaced by forgiveness before bitterness sets in.

---

2   Songwriters: Beth and Matt Redman. Blessed Be Your Name lyrics © Capitol Christian Music Group. Extracted on 15/03/2019 from https://genius.com/Matt-redman-blessed-be-your-name-lyrics

Four

HORTICULTURE

Mary, Mary quite contrary
how does your garden grow?
Yielding well I'm pleased to tell,
as I learn to plant and hoe.
With gumboots on, I potter on
through winter's frost and snow.
But Denmark then becomes too cold,
so, under glass we go.

I was in Europe with two college friends working in the small town of Hørsholm, 26km north of Copenhagen when a nuclear war almost happened. It was October 1962, and with no access to English news we continued to 'plant and hoe with gumboots on' in ignorance of the erupting world crisis. The USA and Russia were facing off over the building of nuclear missile bases in Cuba. The world held its universal breath for 13 long days in what went down in history as the Cuban Crisis.

In Hørsholm, the only breath-holding I was doing related to the chilly morning air of my first Danish autumn. With my two friends, I was more concerned with the simple things of life like getting ourselves to work by 7am.

Our alarm went off ahead of the dawn calls of peacocks roosted above us on the farmhouse roof. Monica was up and almost ready for work and

Hilary was stirring. I stumbled out from the warmth of my doona to switch on the kettle and wait for it to hiss into the quiet of the attic and make our first cup of tea. Shadows crept across the rafters of our dimly lit room as we washed, dressed, ate breakfast and headed out the front door. Another day, another dollar, or Danish Krøne. Monica, Hilary and I were fledgling commercial gardeners spreading our wings in rural Denmark, and as we walked to work in the chill of the morning air, I wondered why I thought this might be fun.

'I think we'll be working on the trees today,' said Monica, walking alongside me.

'I'd rather be in the potting shed,' I replied exhaling a muttering mist of warm breath.

I pushed my hands deep into my duffle coat pockets and wished we'd chosen a job further south where the summer sun lasted longer.

'Come on, we'll be late.' Hilary strode ahead on her long legs, then turned. 'We're over there.' She pointed to our new friend Brian, who was waving from the other side of the road.

'Morning girls.' His broad South African accent cheered me. 'Monica you're with me, lifting. Hilary, you and Audrey are tying.' He knew Monica was the strongest at spadework.

Hilary and I reached the rows and rows of the young cypress trees waiting to be tied, dug up and sold as hedging plants to a long list of customers. The work became so ingrained that I can still recount the process: first, I'd draw the young branches into a wide embrace and then encircle the tree with strong twine. I'd become helpless with my arms grasping the bush and my head pushing into the foliage. A droplet always formed on the tip of my nose and I'd sniff in a way that matched my workmanlike clothes and gumboots. I was a reluctant tree-hugger and my usual good humour rarely rose with the sun.

And nobody knows how cold my toes are growing, tiddly pom. I'd hum to myself, sounding more like grumpy Eeyore than the poetic Winnie the Poo.

'Hurry up please!' my voice wove its way through to Hilary on the other side of the tree.

'Tightening now.' She pulled the twine on the well practised clove hitch knot. 'OK, you can let go,' and I withdrew my embrace. The first tree of the day was restrained and ready to be dug up.

'I wonder how long we'll be doing this?' I stared along the row of trees.

'It's just for this week, I think.' It wasn't, it was several weeks.

Hilary banged her gloved hands together to keep warm, her slim build withstanding the cold better than my more rounded one.

'Can you see Monica and Just Harry?'

We had nicknamed Brian 'Just Harry' because at first he was reluctant to tell us his surname. He was exploring the world like so many young people of the 1960s.

'They're down there.'

Our friends' hard work has produced a huddle of newly lifted trees ready to be taken away.

'OK, next one,' and I hugged the next tree. *I suppose this is what Daddy would have called part of life's rich pattern.*

Trying to look happy while binding trees.

I hope this task has been mechanised since October 1962. It left me with a lifelong dislike of cypress trees and was a far cry from the rich pattern of life I'd envisaged three years before in Kenya. Then I'd planned to work with my father on our Mombasa smallholding growing pineapples, cashew nuts, oranges and hydroponic vegetables. That pipe dream was buried with my father.

Maybe my persistence in the career choice of horticulture was an indicator of my teenage confusion. At the time, I didn't want to do the same as most of my peers, declaring, 'I know what I do NOT want to be; an office worker, nurse or teacher.' My stubbornness brought me into a life of outdoor work in a cold climate and low agricultural wages. I'd realised too late that I would have preferred Kew Gardens or some aspect of plant propagation. In later years God had the last laugh when I found myself teaching nurses and delivering babies; propagation of a different kind.

Monica, Hilary and I had met during our training at Oaklands horticultural college in St Albans, and we were well suited for sharing this year of work and travel. We laughed, discussed life and shared dreams and confidences. If one became irritating or irritated, there'd always be two who could give the other some space. Monica had an intelligent, enquiring mind and a sense of fun that appealed to me. She came from Monmouth on the Welsh border, where her family lived in a rambling Edwardian house filled with family and fox hunting memorabilia. Whenever I visited, I reacted strongly to the animal dander and suffered runny eyes and wheezy cough, even waking one night unable to breathe properly. The family used to kennel the hounds for the local hunt in their now empty stables. The sight of hounds on a kill caused Monica's brother Robert to become a vegetarian. I loved visiting her home and became good friends with Robert. This friendship remained just that, and he eventually married a Malaysian girl and converted to Islam. Monica eventually became a

Buddhist, and I am Christian. The safest Christmas greeting over the years became 'Peace!'

Hilary was an attractive brunette with a quieter nature and committed Christian faith. In contrast to Monica's home, Hilary's was neat and well-ordered. Her parents were Open Brethren, warm and welcoming, but firm about wearing headscarves to church and praying morning and evening. Our treat when we stayed was breakfast in bed; probably so that Hilary's mother could clear the kitchen table and get on with her busy morning. Her father was the headmaster of the local school, and her younger sister, Catherine, went on to study old Icelandic and Norwegian languages. I holidayed with Catherine in Norway in 1965 and enjoyed walking the mountain tracks behind Bergen and travelling the fjords by small boat.

Monica and Hilary eventually married tutors they'd met at college. I was nowhere near ready to marry (not that anyone had asked). I had things to do and places to see.

Training Days prior to Denmark

My college studies were made possible by a financial grant from my mother's home county, Lincolnshire. I attended an interview at their council offices in Boston. As I sat at a large cedar boardroom table opposite the six officials, I felt surprisingly relaxed and confident. Perhaps that was because I was wearing my best light green woollen suit and a pair of new chocolate coloured shoes with matching handbag and gloves. All that was missing were the ubiquitous string of pearls.

'Now then Audrey, why do you want to go to college in Hertfordshire rather than at our county college?' asked the kindly councillor.

'They have broader horticultural training,' I said frankly, if unwisely. They took this in their stride and gave me the grant, somewhat to my surprise.

I completed the prerequisite year's practical experience on an alpine and herbaceous nursery in Twyford, Berkshire, south-west of London. My bed and board were with a retired, straight-laced teacher called Mrs Parrot, who almost immediately confided in me that she'd 'lived in sin' with her now deceased de facto husband. She wasn't so straight-laced after all and I often wondered why she told me so soon in our acquaintance. She also told me she'd failed her driving test four times, which made for some exciting journeys with her as she practised for her fifth test.

I was readjusting to life in England, and caused her great amusement with my naïve questions:

'Well, look at this,' I exclaimed with astonishment one evening. 'This advert is for re-bristling *toilet* brushes – why would anyone do that?' I learnt that these toilet brushes were hair brushes and not the lavatory kind.

'Do you have many chaps on your hands?' she asked one evening as we ate our bread and jam – it was either butter or jam, never both.

'Boyfriends?' I queried throwing her a quizzical look.

'Chilblain; sores from the cold!' This became an ongoing joke between us.

I cycled to work in all weather, but never got chaps on my hands of either sort. During that time I progressed from bicycle to my stepbrothers' handed-down Lambretta motor scooter. The scooter and I never got along, and I ended my relationship with it after I took a tumble into a garden bed of red hot pokers (Kniphofia plants), twisting my right knee. I've stayed with cars, and a bothersome knee, ever since.

At Twyford, I learnt the basics of nursery work and was initiated into the least popular jobs like shovelling rotting compost. I struggled with understanding the broad Berkshire accent of the foreman, but I became sufficiently competent in plant knowledge to advise visitors at London's Chelsea Flower Show. Our nursery's display won a silver award. I was surprised to find our plants needed to be marked up in price when sold in London at the elite Harrods store. Their customers rejected plants at lower prices; it was a strange form of snobbery.

During that year of pre-college experience, I lived for a while with the nursery owner, Wendy, and went to church with her in nearby Reading. There I met up with a girl from my year at the Kenya High School who was in England training as a nurse. These chance encounters with the diaspora from Kenya continued throughout life and across several countries.

Wendy and her Irish housekeeper tried valiantly to teach me the finer womanly skills of needlework, rug making and tapestry. I proudly gave a tapestried cushion to my amazed mother that Christmas. On those domestic evenings, my ability to sit and contemplate like my grandfather disturbed them.

'How can you sit and do nothing?' they said. It felt like a reprimand, and probably was. I needed times of quiet reflection to dissect and absorb the day's experiences. I didn't understand this myself, so I'd dutifully learnt to tapestry.

Wendy married during that year, and I mention this because the honour of being her bridesmaid was spoiled by the embarrassment of having to wear an unflattering, blue satin bridesmaid dress.

At 17 years old I declared my independence by paying for six driving lessons in the city of Reading. I passed my test first time and phoned home to tell Mother. My stepbrother answered the phone.

'Hello David, I'm just ringing to tell Mother I've passed my driving test.'

'Good God!' His surprise was genuine because he'd seen my poor driving practice at home the week before. I'm delighted to have scored a goal for the fairer sex. As part of my campaign towards independence, I travelled across London by Underground instead of taking a taxi to meet Mother and Frances. I emerged triumphant from Kings Cross Underground Station to see their impressed faces and didn't tell them that a kind gentleman had helped me find the right platform.

With my prerequisite practical year under my belt and a financial grant, I arrived at Oaklands College in Hertfordshire. The 100 students were predominately young men, though there was a group of ten girls. I learnt to relate comfortably to men as friends and colleagues, and at weekends groups of us visited botanical gardens, museums and art galleries. The college curriculum included a dawn tour of London's Covent Garden Markets. As a gaggle of students, we enjoyed the hustle and bustle of the place, watching the buying and selling of the freshly harvested vegetables and flowers to wholesalers and shop owners. Behind the stalls, men and women haggled prices between gulping steaming hot cups of tea, a cacophony of regional accents filling the air. We dodged around fast-moving crates on hand-pushed trollies, and the scent of the different fruit and flowers followed us. Discarded vegetables, papers and boxes were piled high around the stalls, ready for later disposal or reuse. I'd forgotten that Pop's potato merchant business traded at Covent Garden until I spotted one of his trucks pulling out of the loading bay, delivery completed. I was disappointed to miss saying hello to the driver.

Six of us became lost as we explored further afield and needed to ask a policeman for directions. As he guided us past Bow Street Police Station, a cockney voice called out, 'Don't run 'em all in, Gov!' I felt I'd entered an old film script and wouldn't have been surprised to see Fagin on the street corner keeping his beady eye on his urchin pickpockets darting through the crowds.

'My grandfather was a London bobby,' I began, but my hesitant opening conversation was lost in the surrounding hub-bub.

Our course continued for a year, and we learnt how to grow, manage and harvest crops. Our weekly tests taught us to identify plants, flowers, pests and diseases. On the practical front, I learnt to reverse a tractor (not very well), make a nut and bolt (I'm not sure why) and understand how a piston engine works, by which time the rest of the class had progressed beyond me. However, I won a prize for bookkeeping. I became used to wearing gumboots, working outside in all seasons and trying to keep my nails clean. All of which was put to some use in Denmark once I'd gained a National Certificate in Commercial Horticulture.

Denmark

All my college-based knowledge was redundant as I greeted the dawn and tied up cypress trees with Monica, Hilary and Just Harry that winter of 1962. We were discovering the realities of being part of a foreign workforce and being unaware of world events like the Cuban Crisis. At weekends we visited other parts of Denmark's Zealand. I was laid up with fluid effusion from my old knee injury when a journey to Sweden was suggested.

'You go,' I said, trying to be generous as my knee ballooned, forcing me to keep off it. I lay on my bed reading and feeling sorry for myself while Hilary, Monica and Just Harry took the ferry to Helsingborg, Sweden. This was a popular place for Danes to shop at lower prices. They had a great time, and I wished they'd not; disappointment smothered any generosity of heart.

Winter approached fast and we increased our efforts to find a warmer workplace. We found this at a wholesale nursery in Avedøre, a southern suburb of Copenhagen. It was a well-known nursery that grew carnation cuttings under glass. They imported disease-free cuttings from their South African nursery.

We said goodbye to the nursery and attic in Hørsholm and found a room to rent in a Danish family's home. It was within walking distance of work. The couple had recently returned from life in Tanzania and my Kenya background helped to persuade them to let us have one room with three bunk beds and use of the bathroom. We had meals delivered, a popular service we had used in Hørsholm, and tried to keep out of the way of the household, except for the occasional chat. This move proved to be wise as the winter of 1962-63 became exceptionally bleak and cold.

The three of us were pleased with the opportunity to learn something of the practices of carnation growing and Stormly Hansen's nursery was the leader in the field. The company's centre in Copenhagen had five large modern glasshouses that functioned like factories. We were treated well and shown the processes of each section. I made a new workmate friend called Kirsten.

'*God morgen,* Audrey.' She would greet me in Danish and I would greet her with an informal Danish greeting: '*Hi,* Kirsten.' This *hi* was not an Americanism.

Workers wore *traesko,* wooden Danish clogs, which kept our feet out of the pools of chilly water on the concrete floor of the glasshouse. These shoes were surprisingly comfortable and gave me more height to work at the aluminium potting benches that stretched the length of the building.

'What are we doing today?' I asked.

'T*rimning*' (trimming) said the English foreman, who had married a Dane and spoke the language. Many Danish words are like old English or Scottish words, and I found this helpful. For instance, the word for church is kirk. The Danish language uses unattractive guttural sounds that use the back of the throat, and I found these near impossible to replicate. The Danes love to practise their English and these things combined to discourage our language learning; that was my excuse anyway. I spoke to Kirsten in English which she understood, and she responded in Danish which I deciphered to get the gist of what she said. We communicated without any major misunderstandings. In later years we met up in London where Kirsten went to work as an au pair. She learned to speak excellent English.

On those mornings in the glasshouse, the local radio station would blast out favourite pop songs in European languages. The core group of workers were local women and no different to many I'd met when working in English nurseries. They were a friendly group who chatted about their families, had the occasional moan, supported one another through good and bad times and rarely argued. They lost no time beginning work when the siren sounded as this was piece work. We were each paid by the number of bundles we trimmed or stuck each day.

These tasks became another set of processes I long remembered: remove a wet bunch of carnation cuttings from the first bucket of the day; using a sharp blade, neatly trim the end of each cutting; return the bunch to my bucket. The following week we might change jobs to '*stikning*' (sticking) where we'd stick the trimmed cuttings into the white, inorganic perlite on the long bench tops. I learnt to hold a bundle loosely in my left hand, pull a cutting through my fingers and stick it into the white perlite in a neat row. This task became one fluid movement in a rhythm of *extract-stretch-bend, extract-stretch-bend* as I stretched to the centre of the bench and worked back to the edge. The rooted cuttings were progressed in another glasshouse before being packed and sold.

Sticking.

'This is a bad winter,' said Kirsten during a lunch break, and I agreed.

'On Saturday we walked on the sea, and even the little waves were solid ice!' We'd found it a strange sensation, similar to walking over a frosty ploughed field. But we could say we'd walked on water.

'You want to come into the city with me on Saturday?'

'OK.'

We travelled by train and went around the shops. People spoke to me in Danish because of my fair looks and I was ashamed not to know the language. The country's history and culture was so much more than stories of Vikings, and we only scraped the surface in our time there.

Christmas approached, and we all travelled into the city to see the street decorations and shop windows that were filled with magical scenes. We were given our first Advent calendars with the little Danish gifts under each date. Our social life improved and we were invited by Danish university students to a long pre-Christmas dinner, where much schnapps was drunk.

'Prost!' we shouted as we toasted something or someone (anything) and down went another small glass of the clear lethal liquid. Two gulps were all I could manage before I felt what one of my aunts would term, 'Very nicely thank you'. We attended a Brethren church several times, courtesy of a letter of introduction from Hilary's parents, and were invited to celebrate Christmas Eve with a church elder and his family.

On Christmas Eve the shops were busy until 5pm when the population headed home to celebrate with their families. I felt I was living in a large Christmas card with the snow on the ground 'deep and crisp and even'. The Danish winter decor matches their love of red and white. Advent wreaths included painted pixies, and candles were lit every day. Everyone looked forward to *Yul* eve when families gave gifts and played games before having an enormous meal of roast pork, boiled potatoes, red cabbage and gravy. We joined in this evening with our Brethren friends, downing the feast with the best of them. There were ten of us around the large table which, with the tree and presents, took up much of the space in the room. We were told that the big treat, and final delight of the evening was a dessert called ris à l'amande. To our initial disappointment, this turned out to be cold, creamy rice pudding. Then hot cherry sauce made with vanilla and almond slivers was poured over the rice and at this point, we delved in.

'What are we looking for?' Monica asked noticing the family eating each mouthful with great deliberation.

'Almonds are hiding in the rice, and we must keep eating until someone finds an almond. The first person to find an almond gets a prize.'

We joined in the careful eating until we discovered that the purpose was to delay finding the almond. Once an almond was found everyone had to stop eating. The first person to find an almond would keep quiet about it so that we could eat more. There was much hilarity as they accused one another of finding and hiding an almond. The evening continued with eating, eating, eating. We were given a lift home about 10pm and hauled our bloated bodies onto our bunks.

'Just as well they're a good Brethren family. Schnapps on top of all that would have finished me!' I groaned. Hilary and Monica grunted as we fell into an uncomfortable sleep. We woke to a peaceful Christmas Day somewhat like our Boxing Day, except for church attendance.

The New Year celebration was quiet for us, and the winter weather continued. I unexpectedly met another Kenya High School friend, Lisa Larsen.

She was there studying. We were pleased to see one another. Monica, Hilary and I hunkered down in our rented room and began to plot our next adventure, a tour of Europe. We decided to travel by bicycle because we couldn't afford anything else that would carry three of us. A cycle ride was just what we all needed to work off the Danish pastries and our winter diet.

We had tolerated our close living quarters remarkably well, with no significant fallings out. As spring approached Hilary was missing Ray, whom she later married, and sat on her top bunk writing letters. Monica and I weren't missing anyone in quite the same way and wrote to friends and family. Back in England, Frances married a German chef called Max in the pretty riverside town of Marlow in Berkshire. Mother continued to stay with Pop. When the Danish icy temperatures rose above freezing, we visited a shop owned by a previous Olympic medallist and bought men's sports bicycles that were strong, yet light. I never quite mastered the multiple gears as we cycled to and from work, preparing our bodies for our Grand Tour. We were tired of the cold and the cutting and sticking and ready for a new adventure. In May 1963 we packed our paniers and saddle bags, waved goodbye and headed south. It was late spring before Monica wrote in her diary, 'Today Audrey removed her vest!' As pretty as the Danish white winter looked, it didn't teach me to like the cold.

Reflection

Looking back on this year it feels like an interlude; a semicolon perhaps. It gave me space away from the call of family crises to be myself, enjoy good friendships and see another country. 'He leads me beside still waters,' Psalm 23. It occurs to me that 'still waters' can also ice up, as they did in Denmark. I began to thaw emotionally.

Five

THE GRAND TOUR

Collectively we, a power of three,
go cycling around, and so confound
all those we see.
We speak no language but our own.
Cobbles shake us to the bone.
It's all good fun in a cyclical way,
on tour in Europe, beginning in May.

A gentle rain trickled down our waterproof cycle capes as we negotiated the mid-morning traffic out of Avedøre, Copenhagen and headed south into the spring greening of the open countryside. Three young women riding men's bikes were an unusual sight for Europe's road users in 1963, and we received some cheerful honking of horns from passing cars. The freedom of the open road felt good, and we kept a steady pace, helped by a following wind. I began to feel quite the adventurer and sniff the air like an animal released from a cage.

Setting off from Avedøre.

Our route was planned around the location of youth hostels, and the Youth Hostel Association (YHA) Handbook was an invaluable guide for our route south. We'd also purchased detailed maps so we could keep to smaller roads as we rode from hostel to hostel. We were delighted when we discovered most hostel managers excused us, as cyclists, from the usual morning chores to allow us to get an early start. Most hostel guests hitchhiked or drove.

The first Danish youth hostel was opening for the season as we arrived and we had the facilities to ourselves. I chortled to myself at the name Niagara inscribed on the antique pull-to-flush toilet cistern. I'm easily amused. The following day our ride to Zealand's south coast took us across Stor Strommen, the longest bridge in Europe at that time. Battling strong winds extended our crossing time to fifteen minutes, and so we began to learn some of the snags about cycling in all weather. The following evening I learned something else.

'My behind and thighs are so sore,' I said, walking bandy-legged like a jockey to our room in Nykøbing Youth Hostel that overlooked the Baltic Sea.

'Mine aren't too bad,' said Hilary.

'Nor mine, take some of my extra wadding if you like,' offered Monica, pulling it out of her saddlebag. She'd been the first to work out the best way to add foam padding to her saddle. I accepted it with a painful smile and praised her forethought. We'd almost beaten the initial stage of aching muscles and saddle soreness by the end of the first week. Come the 21st century, cyclists could buy specially padded pants that minimise this problem. We travelled with less comfort in 1963.

The grand tour

Northern Germany

The ferry from Denmark to Germany left from nearby Gedser, and we almost missed it because of headwinds. Once on board we had our passports stamped, changed some money and disembarked promptly at the docks outside Rostock, Germany. Border crossings were generally easy throughout our travels during this period before the Common Market and later European Union. We were never searched, just treated as a British curiosity and waved on with wry amusement by relaxed customs men. A search would only have uncovered a change of clothes and one plate, one spoon, one mug and a small knife in our panniers. Our saddle bags stored practical things like puncture kits, toiletries and cycle cape. We wore money belts.

Our guidebook showed Rostock to be a thriving, strategically placed city for East German commerce and trade. It also boasted one of the earliest universities in Europe, founded in 1419. Despite its attractions, we decided not to linger there if we were to reach our first German youth hostel by evening. I was unaware then that Schleswig-Holstein to our west was the birthplace of my new brother-in-law Max. His surname is more Scandinavian than German as his ancestral place in the world was a fishing village close to the historically changing border between Germany and the Jutland peninsula of Denmark.

Our plan to travel the smaller country roads worked well, until we hit the cobbled streets of some smaller towns. They shook and rattled us and our bikes and we learnt to be very careful on them. During our first weeks we slipped into a sort of routine and mostly covered comfortable distances between hostels. We enjoyed cycling through the countryside, towns and villages that were well away from the tourist routes. It gave us a feel for people's daily lives as we passed women chatting and shopping and school children playing. We commented on the changing colours of the farmland with their sprouting crops, and we pedalled quickly past pungent farmyard smells and unfriendly geese. My notes of the time listed a few of the spring plants we saw but as the journey lengthened my notes dwindled. I recall mainly flat roads and neat planted fields with fewer hedgerows than Britain at that time. These small havens of German village life challenged our poor linguistic and mime skills. Throughout our travels we managed to convey, 'Three Coca-Colas and a loaf of bread please,' in most places, confusing shopkeepers across Europe with random requests for items like toothpaste.

'Aren't you glad we don't need to ask for toilet paper?' and we joined in the laughter after a unique, and successful piece of mime by Monica who needed toothpaste for her false teeth. Monica and her brother had opted to have all their cavity-ridden teeth extracted when they reached sixteen. I was surprised a dentist would offer to do this.

We continued our trip across the northern part of Germany, avoiding the main roads and staying overnight in towns. Hilary kept the best diary, recorded where we visited and noted our daily distances. We were doing well as we cycled into the small German town of Bad Oldesloe. There our YHA guidebook let us down; the youth hostel had been closed for about a year. We'd cycled 80km, it was five in the evening and too late to go to the next town.

'There's the police station over there,' Hilary said pointing to a sign saying *Polizi* on a building across the wide town square. 'Let's ask if there's somewhere else we can stay.'

We pushed our bikes across the cobbles to the *Polizi* and Monica volunteered to go in and ask. She emerged a few minutes later, smiling to tell us that the police were very helpful and were phoning someone. The policeman came out of the station and beckoned, 'Come.' We left our bikes under police protection and clambered into the police van. He pulled up in front of a busy transport café, and we trailed in after him like three ducklings following their mother. Curious faces turned to stare and the noisy cafe became a hum of interest. At small tables were groups of workers enjoying their lager to the tantalising aroma of fried food. A woman, pretty in a tired way, indicated with a smile for us to come with her. We thanked our policeman friend profusely, '*Vielen Dank.*' We were collecting a few words of German.

'I vill come i' morgen,' he said in a sort of English and we trailed after our hostess behind the counter and carried our bags up the wooden stairs. We were delighted to find a large room with three beds covered with crisp white doonas and a small bathroom along the corridor. Whatever this might cost, we were happy to find safe-haven for the night. After a hearty meal, we snuggled into freshly laundered sheets and the soft warmth of our doonas, and were lulled to sleep by the sound of clinking glasses and chatter rising from the bar below.

In the morning we asked how much to pay, and our hostess says, '*Nichts*,' which puzzled us until we asked our policeman.

'How much to pay?'

'Nichts. Nil. Stadt, town pay.' He shook his head and smiled, 'Nichts hostel, town pay.'

Our faces were probably a picture of surprise, but he insisted.

'*Vielen dank, vielen dank*,' we shook his hand and marvelled at the kindness we received in this small town.

We headed to Hamburg where we stayed one night and which I was glad to leave. It felt unsafe to me with too many loitering men around the city streets and we were too obvious with our bikes. We were three days from the Dutch border, and as we reached the border into the Netherlands at Denekamp it had been ten days since we'd cycled out of Copenhagen. We'd had a few adventures but no punctures or injuries. During our travels through Germany I'd expected more people to allude to the war or be unfriendly, but we experienced only kindness and courtesy. This was explained in part in later years when Frances and I watched old war films on the television with Max. Strangely, he liked these films and we discovered that most Germans of our generation were told almost nothing about the war as they grew up, unlike our childhood tales from Father. The horrors of war are best forgotten, although the death of family members is remembered.

The Netherlands

Cycling in Holland reminded us of our first Denmark experience of battling strong winds, although Holland's flat roads were some compensation. Aalsmeer, 13km south-west of Amsterdam, was sometimes referred to as the flower capital of the world because the world's largest flower auction was based there, along with numerous nurseries. We were met by our college friends, Ray and Pete, who worked at a pot plant nursery and had arranged work for us. Unfortunately, a downturn in work at the nursery reduced the time we were able to work there. The boys had done us proud by arranging for Hilary and I to stay with a Dutch family and Monica stayed with a couple over the road. We were greeted warmly by our hosts and briefly met their two children. They had little English, and once again we needed to speak plainly. I was encouraged to find that the Afrikaans I heard in Kenya gave me clues about some of the words. Danish and German words also helped as these northern languages have similar roots.

We found ourselves living on a polder several metres below sea level. Polders are reclaimed land where the sea is held back by massive dykes. I imagined a line of little boys with their fingers in the dyke walls, like the old story of Haarlem being saved from flooding by one such small boy. But of course, that was not necessary with 20th century engineering, at least so I hoped. There was a canal flowing alongside the main road that ran above the level of our cul-de-sac. I was somewhat disconcerted on our first morning as I looked out of our bedroom window. There was a yacht sailing by at roof level.

We rarely saw our host's children and weren't sure why. We all ate together on the first evening, and although Hilary and I were on our best behaviour, we never ate with the children again. We would eat later, sometimes with the parents and at other times on our own. We wondered if something about our good English table manners distressed them. They were too polite to say and we were too shy to ask. Maybe it simply made it easier for a busy family. Every evening the mother brought us each a large glass of yoghurt covered with hundreds and thousands. Yoghurt hadn't hit the supermarkets in England and it was an enjoyable new taste. We all put on weight in Holland. Monica had a better time with her hosts who spoke more English and enjoyed her company. It seemed to be customary not to draw curtains at night and we could see families living out their lives in full view of their neighbours, unlike Britain where privacy and reserve ruled.

The Flower Auction

We visited the flower auction when the tulips were almost over and the spring flowers were beginning to fade.

'We'll pick you up early tomorrow morning to catch the end of the auction,' said Ray. 'We can use the nursery's van.'

'OK, we'll walk up to the main road' (up to sea level).

The *Aalsmeer Veiling* (pronounced fyling) was one of two important flower auctions in the area. It was a fascinating place with barges loaded with flowers arriving by canal into the heart of the precinct to be auctioned. After the sale some flowers were taken away on barges and others went by road. The central focus of the auction hall was a gigantic clock that timed the fast bidding. Outside Holland this system is called a Dutch auction, where the prices begin high and work their way down. Bidders had only a few seconds to bid on the flowers before the hammer fell. The plants were moved in and out quickly with their bright colours and spring scents exciting the senses. The auction's orderly and efficient processes impressed us.

'A bit different to Covent Garden, isn't it?' I remarked to Monica, recalling the noisy, bustling and chaotic appearance of Covent Garden vegetable, fruit and flower market.

As I write this years later, I feel privileged to have seen the original site of this *veiling*. Since 1963 it has amalgamated with another auction house and moved to much larger premises. Its sale prices influence the price of flowers worldwide.

Amsterdam

One more event in Holland is memorable, and that was our visit with the boys to Amsterdam and its attractions. We travelled by boat on the canal, passing Anne Frank's house and visiting Van Gogh's museum. We were taken unawares into the 'red light' district of the city and at first I thought the women sitting in their windows was another version of the Dutch not drawing their curtains. I was puzzled and naïve about such matters, but as night fell the penny dropped. I noticed young children playing outside these houses. They were a sobering sight and I wondered about their lives, what brought them here and what the future would hold for them. I didn't want to be there, and we asked the boys to take us back into the city centre. The experience stayed with me and I was reminded of it about fifteen years later when I travelled past a similar street in Kalgoorlie, Western Australia.

On one of our trips into Amsterdam we chatted with a man sitting at Amsterdam's central railway station. He recounted his war memories with some urgency and kept asserting that he'd not been a German collaborator during the occupation. A similar explosion of wartime regrets was landed on me later in Frankfurt, where a man was at pains to explain himself. Years later I realised these men needed more profound healing for their wartime trauma than any uncomprehending listener like myself could offer. I saw them as ordinary people misled or pushed into a war not of their own making.

Our time in Holland passed quickly with all our activities and sightseeing. Time was running out for us to be at our next job in Switzerland and we accepted the offer of a lift to Frankfurt with our new German friend Dieter, who was rather keen on Hilary. We sent our bikes ahead by train and crammed into his tightly packed orange Volkswagen. At Arnhem, we joined the road that ran along the River Rhine for the next 400km. The German border crossing was uneventful as curious guards checked our passports and waved us through customs. Dieter looked surprisingly relieved as we drove on and later confessed that our presence had distracted the customs officers, as he'd hoped.

'Why?'

'Coffee is cheap in the Nederland.' His grin almost met his cheeky eyes.

He showed us his stash of Dutch coffee tucked away behind our luggage. We forgave him, and he was a useful guide, pointing out all the attractions and history of places in his broken English as we drove alongside the River Rhine. This saved us time and 480km of pedal power although it was a pity we missed having a closer look at the fairytale castles that lent a contrasting air of romance to the busy road and river highways.

Southern Germany

It took less time than expected to reach Frankfurt where we stayed several days before heading off again. I was pleased to get out of the city as we collected our bikes from the station and headed further south to Heidelberg, then Baden-Baden. This pretty spa town was on the edge of the Black Forest, once dense with spruce, fir, oak and larch trees. The cycle climb into the ancient Black Forest with its deep valleys was a challenge, and on our first day in the forest we pushed our bikes more often than we rode. It rained and we sat on a grassy knoll under a tree sheltering under our cycle capes to eat bread and cheese and have a drink. We tried to cheer ourselves up with weak jokes but we were tired, wet and miserable. The day was saved by a passing truck driver who gave us a lift to the top of a hill. What a relief! We continued our journey up and down some beautiful forest hills and glades for three days, always glad to fall into bed at night. My favourite place was Titisee, about 30km east of the university city of Freiburg and on the north shore of Lake Titisee, about 850 feet above sea level. It was, and is still popular in all seasons with summer sailing and water sport and winter skiing and ice skating. Inhaling the fresh fragrances of the forest, we sat sunning ourselves like lizards coming out of winter hibernation. It was June and summer had arrived.

We all agreed this was a favourite spot as we poured over the museum and leaflet information. The whole area seeped history with its ancient architecture, cobbled streets and wooden buildings. It reminded me of my childhood fairy books with tales of ogres and princesses and woodland elves. '*I'm a troll, fol-de-rol,*' I muttered as we pushed our bikes across a small wooden bridge. Hilary and Monica raised their eyebrows at one another. The next day we cycled 75km to Basel and the Swiss border.

Switzerland

Basel central train station is the busiest international border station in Europe. Trains head in and out of it from France, Germany, Italy and Switzerland. Outside its baroque style building was the hub for the city's tramlines, and we approached the station with caution knowing that tramlines are traps for bicycle tyres. The station was well set out despite its age, and we found our way to the ticket office, purchased tickets to Lausanne and found somewhere to eat and wait for our train. Railway stations are wonderful places to people-watch, and there was a buzz of nationalities coming and going in all directions. It was like watching one of my grandfather's hives with the bees flying in with their pollen load, twirl in a dance and head off again.

I was enjoying this scene when we began to be pestered by a group of bored, predatory young Spanish men who decided we would be their entertainment. We dealt with this by ignoring them, slapping hands and eventually getting angry. None of it seemed to work in my case. It was all a game to them and after half an hour I'd had enough. Maybe it was the blonde hair or something else that made me a prime target, but I was determined not to put up with it.

'This is awful,' I said to Hilary and Monica as I pushed another wandering hand off my thigh.

'What's wrong?' My travel companions asked, emerging from their books. They were unaware of the continuing problem I was having as I sat on the end of the bench.

'I'm going to find a guard.' I said, 'I can't stand all this pestering.'

I found a guard who understood immediately and said they often had trouble with groups of itinerant workers. He gathered us up and escorted us to the Waiting Room. He then checked the passport of every man in the room and asked all those with Italian or Spanish passports to leave. To my surprise they went without a murmur.

'Come and get me if you have any more trouble,' the guard said, shutting the waiting room door.

There were several other women in the room and we all smiled at one another before returning to our books. I felt I would like Switzerland.

The train took us to Lausanne on Lake Geneva where we retrieved our bikes from the luggage van and cycled wide-eyed around the Lake to Montreux. Life seemed gentle here; the sun was shimmering on the lake as we passed small cafés with colourful umbrellas perched on the banks of the lake. The sounds of laughter and clinking glasses rose from tables of holidaymakers with their children playing on the grass nearby. It was easier to communicate in this French-speaking landlocked country bordered by five countries and visited by many other nationalities. We stopped for lunch at one of the lakeside cafés to discuss how we would get to Chateau-d'Oex and the small Christian hotel that had agreed to employ us for three weeks. It was in the mountains of this Canton of Vaud, the third largest Swiss canton.

'I wonder if we can cycle up to it?' says Hilary.

'Let's ask,' and we approach a waitress and point to our map.

'Can we cycle to here?'

'Yes,' she says with certainty.

'Is the road very steep?'

'No, not too steep.'

We set off with enthusiasm but the road became steeper and steeper until I was gasping for breath. Obviously steep was a relative term, and 'very steep' meant something entirely different to people who lived among mountains. We were walking next to the railway line and we heard a train toot as it approached. I waved it down, not expecting it to stop and was delighted when is slowed to a halt alongside us. We hopped on board with our bikes, acknowledging the knowing smiles of the passengers. This move was in the nick of time as the road soon petered out and we entered a long rail tunnel. The train then climbed to an altitude of 958m (3143 feet). Our informant was wrong, we could not cycle to Chateau-d'Oex from our starting point.

Chateau-d'Oex

The sun shone on fertile green fields in that ancient alpine village nestled between the mountains; a small Shangri-La of farms and hospitality. The sound of cow bells marked out the Simmental cattle grazing freely in lush pasture painted with pastel hues of white and yellow flowers. This was a picture from the childhood classic, *Heidi*. The people of this Canton had strong connections with England that went back to their open hospitality and care of wounded World War I prisoners, from both sides of the conflict.

We left the station and found our way to the hotel where we were greeted with much interest before being shown to the staff quarters. We learnt later we were not quite the robust, muscular women the young staff members had joked about before our arrival, referring to us as the 'Three British Tanks'. Well, really! Hilary and Monica began work as housemaids the next day and I was relegated to the kitchen, where I became chief washer-upper in charge of the sink and large dishwasher. I wondered what this work allocation assumed about our various abilities, and I was never game to ask. I became what in Kenya we would have called a 'kitchen toto' or little kitchen helper. I did an efficient job and resigned myself to being 'below stairs' for the duration. I enjoyed my time there.

'Come along, my little rabbit, it's lunchtime,' said Hennie, the tall young Dutch cook who appreciated my enjoyment of his salads.

About 50 cheerful English guests arrived from mainly English Brethren churches and we discovered that the Brethren Church had a long-standing ministry and connection with the area. This explained how Hilary's parents found us the work there. In the evenings the guests had lectures and we were free to explore. The owner's son, Michael, was a dangerously fast skier in the winter, according to his concerned parents. He was another of Hilary's admirers and with Hennie, our cook, they showed us around the valley and explained some of its history and sights.

'See these caves?' said Michael. 'Secret stashes of high-powered weapons are hidden in them. And every Swiss man has a gun that he must keep oiled and ready, and the military can arrive for an inspection at any time with no warning.'

'Is this because you're a neutral country?' My interest was piqued and I peered into the gloom from the cave's entrance.

'Yes, but we're also a small country bordered by big powers – Germany, Austria, Italy and France.' I decided that the precision that makes the Swiss famous for its watches, applies to much more of their life, and I admired them for it. I also found it somewhat intimidating and wondered if the shadows of war would ever diminish in the lives of humanity.

It was my twentieth birthday, and there was a special treat in store, a genuine Swiss fondue. Our new friends took us to a small unassuming restaurant and seemed to enjoy instructing us.

'We'll have cheese fondue, but you must never drink anything but white wine with it.'

'Why?'

'Any other cold drink makes the cheese harden into a ball in your stomach, and then it can't pass through your gut.'

We needed no persuading to drink white wine, and I enjoyed a happy 20ᵗʰ birthday with good friends, marking the end of my teenage years. Mostly I was pleased to leave those years behind.

Our time in Chateaux-d'Oex came to an end far too quickly. We had fun and our lives had been exposed to different people, cultures and places. It was time to resume our Grand Tour. The plan was to continue into France and Spain before heading north-west through France to England. But Monica had been quietly thinking about her future.

'I've decided to cut my losses and go back home and not come to France with you,' she said. 'I'd rather keep the money I've saved. I'm thinking of joining the police force.'

Although this was a surprise, we supported Monica's decision. I could see Monica being a level-headed policewoman, and as it turned out, she was in the force for several years before she married David, the Oaklands College tutor and returned to horticulture. She told me a few years later that the hardest part of policing was keeping her feet free of blisters because of all the foot patrols. Monica tried to persuade us to return with her but neither Hilary nor I were ready to leave. I was still finding the journey fascinating and Hilary felt this could be her only chance to see more of Europe. We opted to continue our tour but travel with Monica to Geneva. We said goodbye to our friends in Chateau-d'Oex and headed to Geneva, soaking up the panoramic scenery as we descended via a different route to Montreux. The cycle ride around the Lake to Geneva was relaxing and we spent our last two days together looking around the city. Monica then boarded the train to Paris and we felt we had a piece missing after being a threesome for so long. The next day we bought tickets to Narbonne in France, took our bikes to the station and waited for the train. We were wiser about mountain roads and didn't even consider cycling out of Switzerland. It was early July and two months since we left Denmark.

France

The last section of our grand tour had its moments. Exasperation made me unusually fluent in high school French when our bikes were still missing a day after we arrived in Narbonne.

'*Trouvez mes bicyclettes. Vite, vite!* I waved my arms around in true Gallic fashion.

I'm sure they chuckled later and may not have understood my French, but they appreciated the sentiment and found our bikes the next day. We had arrived at 4am and, as in Germany, we appealed to the police, who found us a room for the two nights. There we closeted ourselves until the bikes arrived. Hilary and I soon became aware that as two, instead of three young women, we were more vulnerable. We travelled fewer back roads to reach the busy seaside town of Perpignan and one night in the town's crowded youth hostel was enough for us.

'Let's get to Cerbere. It looks like a pretty coast road, and the hills can't be *that* hard,' Hilary suggested.

I agreed.

Off we cycled across the foothills of the Pyrenees to relearn our Swiss lesson about hill gradients. As we rode along, we were serenaded by the shrill tunes of cicadas sitting in the roadside shrubbery, and the road ahead shimmered in the heat. We struggled with the heat and hills, and stopped frequently to catch our breath and admire the view of craggy hillsides planted with olive trees. There was little traffic as we wound our way around the rugged clifftops imagining the joy of plunging into the unreachable clear, crisp blue of the distant Mediterranean Sea.

'That is so inviting,' Hilary said, pointing to the cove below that nestled the fishing village of Cerbere. We rode quickly past the ugly railway terminus – Cebere was the main rail connection with Barcelona, and where the French rail gauge changed to that of Spain. In the large shunting yard discarded axles were lying around a complex interchange of lines. This was not what interested us and we kept our heads down as we headed downhill to the beach. We were exhausted and hungry.

'Let's find a hotel and stay awhile.' Another good suggestion from Hilary. 'This hotel looks reasonable, and we can afford it.' I thought this was a great idea. We stayed for two days at the small seafront Hotel Dorade, where we luxuriated in the sea and sunbathed in the warmth of summer sunshine. We felt profligate spending our hard-earned money, but decided we deserved the rest before we tackled Spain, bearing in mind our experiences of Basel central station.

Spain in a Day

Our intended destination was Barcelona and we left Cerbere in the cool of the early morning. We'd agreed that neither of us wanted to see a bullfight.

'Hil, do you remember the song 'Little White Bull' that Tommy Steel put out?'

I'd liked Tommy Steele's songs when I was a young teenager in Nairobi. Hilary hadn't heard it.

'What about 'Torero'? You know, it goes like this: *I met him on a bus in Barcelona.*' I intoned the only line I could remember.

'Ha, ha,' she laughed. 'We'd better not get on any buses then.' Little did we know that we wouldn't get to Barcelona.

The conversation ended as we pushed our bikes up the next rise. A lorry driver stopped and offered us a lift to the Spanish border and we hopped on with alacrity. From the border we cycled up and down hills in the increasing warmth of the day, enjoying the beauty of the countryside with its Mediterranean backdrop. As the land flattened out, the road took us away from the coast and there was a marked difference in our surroundings. There were stretches of road lined with squalid shacks, empty bottles and tins, broken glass and general detritus. Life was rough and tough for these people. We realised we were back in the world of male harassment and even the policemen were a nuisance. When I had a puncture, we felt it necessary to dodge behind a bush to mend it. At lunchtime we paused in the town of Figueres in the province of Girona to buy food and drink. We were unaware that this was the birthplace of the artist Salvador Dalí or we may have stayed longer. As it was, we decided we'd bitten off more than we could chew on this section of our Grand Tour, and we would return to the comparative safety of France. So, it was back to Perpignan. We were probably more ready to head home than we'd previously acknowledged.

I had a second puncture 6km from the nearest garage, but we were directed to a bike repair man in the nearby village who replaced the inner tube. It was siesta time and the town streets were quiet as people rested during the heat of the day. It was not our choice to be out in the midday sun like mad dogs and Englishmen, but we needed to get back to France before nightfall. Once again, we crossed the Pyrenees.

'Phew, this is steep but not as steep as Switzerland,' Hilary said as we cycled and walked our way back to France.

'Only another twenty kilometres.'

'Here comes the rain.'

'I'm not putting my cape on, it's too hot.'

'I agree.'

France to England

It was still daylight at 8.15pm when we reached Perpignan, having cycled 117km in our determination to return to France. We were very proud of our effort and rewarded ourselves with the next day at the beach before we caught the train to Orleans in the Loire Valley. We entered that city early the next morning much more peaceably than the city's famous heroine, Joan of Arc. She had entered in 1429 when she was only a year younger than Hilary and me. Her visions led her to ride into Orleans on a horse and defeat the English in battle. The major differences between her entry and ours were that we were English, riding bicycles, yet to have any visions and the only battle we might have anticipated was if our bikes had not arrived on the train with us. The bikes had arrived safely and we rode on to the city of Chartres.

The youth hostel in Chartres was crowded but we found beds in a large dormitory. Hilary was woken when a voice said 'Bonsoir'. The speaker was an African boy settling onto the end bunk near the dormitory door. Hilary told me about him the next morning.

'Last night, Audrey, I woke up when the African boy arrived back, and then I woke up again later. He was tucking you up in a blanket, and then he tucked me up too and said it was cold. It was very odd.'

'Really? I don't remember a thing. It's good you woke up. I expect he was being kind.'

But we never knew for sure, as we'd become more wary over the last few weeks. We rode out of Chartres on July 14 in the rain. The following night in Evreux the hostel was cold, and we were disturbed by the door opening and lights going on and off. The hostels were in their busy summer season. We were pleased to be on the last leg of our journey home.

It was mid-summer and France was awash with holidaymakers. We knew we'd missed opportunities to see more of France, but we'd been away from our families almost a year and like ponies on the homeward trot, we sped up. We pushed ourselves to ride longer distances, cycling 109km on our final day in France. Our legs were like jelly as we paused for lunch in Rouen. That evening we reached the port city of Dieppe where the ferry across the English Channel (La Manche to the French) was due to leave at 10pm.

'Come on Audrey, we'll get tickets and put our bikes in, then we can look around town.'

'This place reminds me of English seaside towns. Look they even sell fish and chips over there.'

We boarded later that evening to find seats and slept through the whole crossing. At 5am, we woke up, had a coffee and disembarked in Newhaven, Surrey. We passed through customs and looked for our bikes.

'Oh no, not again!' we chorused.

Sure enough, they hadn't arrived with us and we had an eight-hour wait for the next ferry to bring them. We stayed overnight at an Inn on the edge of Ashdown Forest before setting out for Hilary's home in Croxley Green, Hertfordshire. We negotiated cycling through London and arrived at Croxley Green triumphant and unexpected at four o'clock, in time for tea. It was the 17th of July 1963 and we'd cycled about 2600km (about 1610 miles) in three months.

The decision to surprise our parents worked well for Hilary, but less so for me. The following day Hilary's parents drove me with my bicycle north on the A40 and I cycled the last 15 miles to Frampton. I arrived unannounced around 4pm and Mother tried to be pleased to see me, but was 'all of a dither'. I should have realised that a surprise was not the best thing for her and I could have made things difficult for her with Pop. I felt sick in the pit of my stomach; I was home.

As a result of my time in Denmark and on tour, Mother began to accept my growing maturity and I felt her loosening some inner maternal tie. As if to mark my new self-assurance, I sold my bike locally for the same amount I'd bought it for originally. Hilary, Monica and I, as a band of three, had lived together for twelve months and we remained friends always, even as our lives took divergent paths. Hilary's note-taking has helped me reconstruct this account. But where to from here? I knew horticulture wouldn't suit me as a lifelong career. As I visited friends around the country, the idea of nursing took hold. I thought I might give it a go and leave if I didn't like it, and this casual thought sowed the seed of what became a 40-year career that took me to more interesting places.

Reflection

My experience in Europe taught me many things, not least that I was more capable than I realised and that people and places were fascinating. Perhaps I should have been an anthropologist. The journey led to my preference for living in other countries, rather than travelling as a tourist. I find it hard to believe I was once able to cycle those distances. Hindsight also shows me how protected we were by our parents' covering prayers, especially when Hilary and I travelled the last part together. I'm sad that it's too late to thank them.

'Though one may be overpowered, two can defend themselves.
A cord of three strands is not quickly broken.' Ecclesiastes 4:12 (NIV)

Six

Nursing Training

Spires in the sunlight
and colleges ancient.
Taking care of every sick patient
in rustling uniforms and hats we starch,
'No running, Nurse, but hurry, quick march.'
*

Moving from bedpans to giving injections,
changing the dressings to deal with infections,
feeling fulfilled when someone is well,
some things are sad or too strange to tell.
*

Three years in Oxford with work and fun,
the world's my oyster when all is done.

Memories swirl in the dust of my nursing years, and I'm taken back to the beginning. I was visiting Wendy, my previous boss and friend on the alpine and herbaceous plant nursery in Berkshire. It was the autumn of 1963 when I returned to England from my year in Europe. This was the year President Kennedy was assassinated and I was in my room when the news broke. Wendy called up to me, 'Audrey, come quickly and listen to this. President John Kennedy's been shot!' I scurried downstairs as Wendy turned on the television.

The events that unfolded on our screen entered the history books as a crime with no satisfactory answers and a plethora of conspiracy theories. Meanwhile, England was still reeling from the Profumo Affair and the discovery of a ring of Soviet spies in the corridors of power, named as Burgess, Maclean and Philby. The Great Train Robbery filled the newspapers for months, but the death of CS Lewis, author of the Narnia series was overshadowed by the American President's murder. Radio Caroline was the first English off-shore pirate radio station, at sea to avoid licence fees, and popular music hits like *She Loves You* by the Beatles, filled the airwaves. And I was deciding whether the new television production of *Dr Who* was intended to be as amusing as I found it.

Events in my life were also unfolding as I explored an alternative career to horticulture. I'd long since recognised my sense of inadequacy around all things medical, and maybe JFK's assassination brought this to the front of my mind again. This feeling of inadequacy probably stemmed from my father's terminal illness more than the sight of murder, but it encouraged me to consider training as a registered nurse. I needed interesting work that would extend me, add life skills and be warm in the winter.

A three-year course, plus one year as a staff nurse seemed like an eternity at age 20, until I rationalised that I would be 23 in three years' time no matter what I did during those years. This was a rather strange rationale that lacked any sense of call or altruism, but it was sufficient to get me into a fulfilling nursing career that spanned forty years. The advantage of hospital-based training was the provision of accommodation and a small wage that gave me financial independence. I chose Oxford to avoid the hustle and bustle of crowded city life in London. I applied to the Radcliffe Infirmary and gained a place in the next intake because someone had dropped out. The Radcliffe was a modern training hospital and most of my group had applied years in advance.

My change of career stood me in good stead and opened my world still wider, enabling me to pick and choose where to travel and live. One unexpected adjustment with nursing was the change from the majority male workforce of horticulture to a mainly female hospital workforce. I'd found working with men less complicated, I disliked the hospital's military-style hierarchy, but I could cope with it. I treated people with due respect, but never addressed men as Sir unless it was their title, sticking with Dr or Mr – it was my small rebellion.

Beginning Experiences

Mother drove me from Lincolnshire to Oxford in the family's Jaguar. I mention the car because it carried a certain amount of status and I was feeling low on status at the time; Christmas at home had been stressful. We parked in front of Arthur Sanctuary House, where I'd live for the next three months at least. It felt like going to boarding school and my stomach was churning. In future years this Headington property and grounds became the site of the John Radcliffe Hospital, but in January 1964 its grounds included a tuberculosis hospital, the nurses' quarters and part of the nursing school. Just as with boarding school, Mother came into the house with me to see me settled. I reported to the Home Sister and was given my room number and keys – upstairs turn right and down the corridor. I was to share with Jenny, the oldest of our group at twenty-four. She was already unpacked and organised as I entered.

'Hello, I'm Jenny. Are you happy to be on that bed?'

'Hello Jenny, I'm Audrey, and this is my Mother. Yes, this bed's fine thanks.'

I walked Mother to the car, and we were both feeling a little strange, like we'd stepped back in time. We said our goodbyes and I returned to unpack and get to know Jenny, who would become a good friend over the next three years. She came from a medical family and had been working as a technician on the heart and lung surgical team at Saint Bartholomew's Hospital in London. She eventually married a teacher from an Oxfordshire private boys' school, and during their courtship (it was very proper) I went to Yorkshire with them to camp with a group of 6th Form boys. I remember this because it snowed, our tent collapsed, and we slept in Jenny's red car, a Morris Mini.

Also, I was paid court by a confident, handsome 16-year-old Greek student, and I'd wished he was a little older.

As budding nurses, we had much to learn, and this came home to us on our first day of Preliminary Training School (PTS). We were gathered in the classroom to learn our first skill, folding our highly starched pleated first-year caps. It was not easy, the second and third-year caps were more straightforward. As we were mastering this essential nursing skill, one of the group fainted. None of us knew what to do and we all felt quite ashamed. Also, I was usually the 'faintee', not the carer. My decision to become a nurse was affirmed.

During those three months of PTS, Miss Flowers, the tutor, taught us to make beds with neat hospital corners, take temperatures, give bedpans and provide all the necessary skills required for our menial first-year duties. We wore a short-sleeve dress, stiff starched apron, starched hat, black stockings (and suspender belts) and black lace-up shoes. We had a brown cape with a red lining to wear outdoors. But we were not allowed to wear our uniforms in public places for reasons of hygiene and always wore our official blue gaberdine coats over our uniform. I liked the uniform, but the starched apron took a bit of getting used to. The underside of one corner of the apron became a handy spot for writing quick reminders in biro.

We were the last group to be sent to cookery classes, but I wished they'd continued as I'd not learned to cook as a child. However, making junket and straining soup had become less of a nursing skill and most of the girls rebelled, ending classes forever. We were on the cusp of a changing paradigm in nursing, and cookery was not to be a part of it. Oxford was a centre of excellence that attracted innovation and research, along with more than its share of rarer medical and surgical conditions.

Student Nurse Payne

I felt excited and nervous the first time we were to accompany a junior nurse on a ward. We were driven by bus down Headington Hill, over Magdalen Bridge into High Street, right turn at Carfax and along St Giles to the southern end of Woodstock Road. The main gates of the Radcliffe led to an imposing stone building, and to get to the front door we skirted around a large fountain of the Greek god Triton, a strange choice for a hospital nowhere near the ocean. The hospital had been opened in 1769 as an infirmary, relying on donations from benefactors and subscriptions for admission rights. The front entrance to the hospital was through heavy, wide double doors typical of many 18th century houses. We were led to the central concourse with high ceilings and a long wide corridor that led to most of the wards. If it had a platform for trains, I wouldn't have been surprised. It felt like a central station. We stood to one side of this hub, a nervous huddle of young girls trying to look like nurses in our crisp uniforms and properly pleated caps. Forty years later this same group reunited from across the globe for a weekend and revisited this site, and I felt a flutter of the same nerves.

My most remembered patient that day was a 35-year-old pregnant woman whose heart condition meant that each pregnancy was life-threatening for her. Her husband didn't believe in birth control and this was her sixth child. I was very challenged and emotional about her predicament as she confided in tears that she hadn't wanted another baby. The doctors were trying to get the husband's consent for her to have a tubal ligation. This did not improve my opinion of marriage and made me realise that medical ethics are not as straightforward as I'd assumed.

I was pleased my first posting after PTS was to the Churchill Hospital, a smaller hospital within the Oxford group. Many of its wards were Nissen buildings thrown up during WWII to provide orthopaedic care for bomb injuries. When this proved unnecessary, the buildings were leased to the United States Army Medical Corp until 1946, when it reopened as a conventional hospital. It was less intimidating than the Radcliffe and I would probably have given up training if I'd started out on a Radcliffe ward. At the Churchill Hospital I encountered benevolent ward sisters who encouraged and supported their student nurses and we lived in a nurses' home that could allocate us a room each. Several of my first experiences remain clear to me.

'Nurse Payne, it's time you gave an injection. Mrs Black is due for her penicillin. Collect the things you need and I'll see you in the clinical room.'

The young ward sister in charge of this medical-neurology ward rolled up her long blue sleeves, took two white ruffs out of her pocket and put them on her arms to cover the ends of her rolled sleeves. I scuttled off to get the items I needed. This was the first item to be signed off as competent in my Experience Manual. I answered the sister's questions.

'Yes sister, it's intramuscular and given in the upper outer quadrant of the buttocks.'

'Why there?'

'It's the best muscle mass and avoids the sciatic nerve.'

The penicillin was a hefty dose of thick white fluid that required a large bore needle. I drew up the required amount in the glass syringe, visually marked out the quadrant, cleaned the skin, and with the concentration of a marksman I pierced the spot. Sister's kindness to the patient, and me, was that Mrs Black was unconscious; to my relief, she remained so. I felt a disproportionate sense of achievement as I told my yet-to-inject friends that this was easier than injecting an orange.

My first embarrassing moment involved my naivety about men's bodies. The men's neurological ward was opposite the women's medical ward where I worked. I was asked to go there to sit with a patient for an hour during the special nurse's lunch break. The man in his 40s was unable to speak or move, which I could cope with until he indicated that he needed a urine bottle. *But now what is he telling me? Put his **what** into the bottle?* With forefinger and thumb I did as asked, treating it like porcelain china. I could see he wasn't amused by my discomfort, which made me feel worse. He had enough to cope with without having a naïve rookie as his nurse. After that, and a few other encounters with bodily functions, I stopped worrying and just got on with whatever was necessary. My stepbrothers commented once that all I saw as a nurse were old men's bodies, and I joked later with a close friend that they never offered to show me an alternative. Not that I wanted them to. I liked my change of career and when asked whether I preferred horticulture or nursing, I'd reply, 'Well there's a bit of muck attached to both.' But horticulture was less confronting.

Although the Radcliffe had a good ethos of care and teaching, it also bred the long-established military culture of obedience without question, and some nurses were unforgiving and uncaring of those of lower rank. Some were even vindictive. Years later, when I was completing a nursing degree, I heard a colleague express this attitude as, 'Nurses eat their young'. I escaped the worst of this by being a few years older than my peers and having more

life experience. One tradition only stopped a year after I entered the profession. This was the need to take any broken thermometers to Matron
Preddy's office and there receive a blistering reprimand. I saw this behaviour
in full flow when a fellow student came to me.

'Audrey, I'm going to leave nursing, will you come with me to tell
matron?' a distressed friend, Kerry, asked me.

She was in tears at the thought of facing up to matron, whom we knew
would upbraid her unmercifully. I agreed, asking her why she was leaving. It
transpired that the unsociable shiftwork was threatening to destroy her relationship with the love of her life. She was an excellent nurse, but the lifestyle
was not for her. I waited outside matron's office wondering if I would hear
raised voices. All was quiet until Kerry emerged ten minutes later.

'Are you alright?' She was subdued as we walked back to the old Victorian
house on Woodstock Road that housed student nurses.

'I'm pleased it's over. She read me the riot act about wasting hospital
time and money and has put me on night duty to work out my notice.' Her
voice gave way to a tremble, and I put my hand on her arm in sympathy.
We knew what this meant, it was like being sent to the salt mines; straight
to night duty and ten shifts of relieving on random short-staffed wards with
all the unpleasant tasks and numerous last offices for patients whose lives
ended at night. These final weeks would banish any doubts Kerry may have
harboured about leaving. It was cruel. The Radcliffe may have been forg-
ing ahead with modern nursing practice, but changing a culture has taken
generations.

Further Experiences

The call went out, 'The Change List is up' and we flocked to the nurses'
noticeboard to check our placement for the coming three months. I had
two stints away from the two main hospitals, one at the TB hospital in the
grounds of Manor House and one at The Slade, a hospital for skin diseases.
I enjoyed both and always found medicine interesting. I enjoyed this area of
nursing and liked learning about diseases and unusual conditions. Others

preferred the fixing-up of bodies through surgery. The only surgical specialty I found interesting was plastic surgery.

In my first year I was more emotional when I nursed cancer patients, especially those with terminal lung cancer, reminding me of my father. The Radcliffe was unique in its approach to terminal care, and when a patient formed a trusting relationship with one or two nurses, we would be allocated to be with that one patient who was dying, even if we were simply sitting and holding his or her hand. The rest of the nursing team would pick up the slack.

I spent one stretch of night duty at the TB hospital where the rooms were kept cool and we were allowed to wear cardigans, normally banned to prevent cross infection. I discovered that we were an unofficial tea-break stop for the police on night patrol in the area. While they sat chatting to the staff nurse, other nurses were known to tie large bows of toilet paper (government supply) around the patrol car's blue light.

Some of the long-stay patients were unique characters and I recall one man who refused all liquids except champagne, which his friend supplied in copious amounts; he eventually died peacefully in an alcoholic haze.

At The Slade Hospital I nursed my first leprosy case, little knowing that in future years I would care for others in north-west Australia. I enjoyed slopping soothing creams onto irritated skins, and helping people into tar baths, but it wasn't a nursing specialty I'd choose.

A new training option of three month's midwifery within our general training became available during our third year and I grabbed the opportunity. My friend Gilly also chose to do this. We were in the same set and became friends in our second year. As students in the maternity wing we did our share of menial tasks, but there was a bonus when cleaning an empty labour ward. Nitrous oxide gas (laughing gas) was available for pain relief during labour in those days, and we enjoyed the euphoria it offered while we cleaned.

The maternity section's labour ward was upstairs from the antenatal outpatient's clinic and the way up with a patient was in an Art Deco-era lift. I discovered the foolishness of this arrangement when I was summoned by the clinic nurse.

'Nurse, I want you to escort Daphne upstairs to the antenatal ward. Here are the notes – and she's in early labour.'

I pushed the wheelchair with 17-year-old Daphne into the ancient lift and rattled shut its black metal gate. We ascended at a smooth, if noisy pace until it suddenly stopped between floors. Agonies of imagined difficult deliveries engulfed me as I made light of the delay with the contracting Daphne. Those ten minutes seemed like a lifetime as I waited for the people below to get help and the lift to resume its journey to the first floor. I thought I was about to learn to deliver a baby the hard way. After this I made sure I had scissors and a cord tie in my pocket, just in case there was a next time.

During my first experience of observing a birth, I disgraced myself by almost fainting. In the overheated room, I concentrated on everything; the nurse's preparation, the groans and reluctant puffing of the mother, until I was overwhelmed, felt faint and had to leave. This happened at the first three deliveries I attended before I finally saw a birth. I found that midwifery was another specialty I could take or leave, and I waited a further ten years before qualifying as a midwife, more out of necessity than desire. It became an essential skill for senior nursing positions in other countries.

Our student nurse pay was about £15 a week and by our third year my flat mates Gilly, Marion and I were getting short of money. We found non-nursing jobs for our one day off a week. Oh, the energy of youth! Gilly and Marion cleaned the home of two university academics.

'Goodness, Audrey, their home is such a mess. Washing up is left for days, and there are toys and books everywhere. It takes half an hour to clear up before we even start hoovering.'

Meanwhile, I had found a gentle gardening job at the home of a keen gardener, where we discussed iris varieties over coffee and did a bit of planting. She was being kind to a nurse and enjoyed the company. I also enjoyed her company, and my first experience of underfloor heating.

Having a car made a big difference in my life. Pop and Mother found a second-hand Ford Anglia to replace my first car, a Volkswagen which I'd crashed into the wall on Headington Hill. I wanted to look after my car properly and was interested in its motor, so when I saw an advertisement for an AA meeting I thought: '*Automobile Association, I'll go to that.*' I entered the town hall and sat at the back. The audience was mainly male and I looked around for signs of vehicles or information on cars. Nothing. I listened to talks, and nothing was said about cars. I left the hall bemused. It was a month later that I heard about Alcoholics Anonymous and realised where I'd been. No wonder there were no cars and I received some strange looks. It made a good story and gave us all a laugh.

39 Chalfont Road

Gilly and I shared a flat here. We could cycle or walk to the Radcliffe or drive if we were running late. Matron allowed us to 'live out' as we were over 21 and in our third year; a new concession in 1966. The flat was on the ground floor of a semi-detached, late-Victorian house and had a large bedroom, sitting room and kitchen which led out to a long narrow garden. My bedroom was in the attic space above the kitchen. This was a cosy nook with a sloping ceiling and a small window looking out onto the back garden. I would climb up a ladder each night and close the trap door on the world. I loved it. Visitors were dragged into the kitchen, passed the terrapin nibbling a lettuce leaf in its waterless aquarium and told, 'Come and see where Audrey sleeps', pointing to the ladder leading to the square hole in the ceiling. It was the showpiece of our home.

Gilly and I had struck up a lifelong friendship during our second year. Neither of us quite fitted the norm of our nursing group. We were a little older, had lived overseas, worked in other occupations and loved literature. Gilly also loved classical music and taught me to love many pieces I had previous rejected. We would go to strange Ingmar Bergman films at the small cinema in Walton Street behind the hospital. It was a popular cinema for hospital staff and beepers were within calling range.

Before nursing training Gilly had worked in a dental surgery in Oxford and socialised with a group of postgraduate students. Some of these young men went on to become well known in their field of animal behaviour. One visitor was Richard Dawkins, who went on to become an ethologist, evolutionary biologist and articulate atheist. My only connection was that he was an admirer of Gilly who was an attractive, intelligent, petite blonde. I found these young university men ignorant about life for all their academic knowledge, but I liked nearly all of them. The most flamboyant was an Indian prince who was in love with Gilly and arrived one afternoon, dressed all in white, including white gloves, to whisk her off somewhere perhaps less exotic than he looked. I believe he eventually returned to India to an arranged marriage. Gilly went on to marry Richard, a mathematician she met later in Leicester, where she qualified as a health visitor.

We needed a third member of the flat to help with the rent, and as Gilly had to share her large bedroom with them, she chose them. First came Marion, one of our nursing group who wanted to marry her sweetheart and live comfortably in the Cotswold's, which she did. Next came Elaine with her quiet artistic nature, who worked at the Radcliffe Eye Hospital as an enrolled nurse. Her State Registered Nurse (SRN) training had been interrupted by the onset of Crohn's Disease. Lastly came Anne, a well-educated, efficient and likeable nurse of our age, who was being groomed by her mother to be a good catch for someone discerning. She was a Cordon Bleu cook, and at the end of our training was sent to Perugia to learn Italian and hone her social skills. She was then happily caught. I became the only one of our trio to remain cheerfully uncaught.

Several ex-Kenya High School friends visited, studied or worked in Oxford. I spent some time with Cynthia Brierly and caught up with her again after I finished training. Sadly, she died too young in a road accident in Kenya. Ebba Castley had married and her husband was studying for a short time in Oxford and I visited them several times. Friend Kay, later known as Kathleen, was travelling the world and settled to work in Oxford as a secretary; she married a solicitor and remained in the area. Friend Joan came to visit when she was training as an orthopaedic nurse and physiotherapist in Shropshire. Several other Kenya friends passed through but I have no memory of Frances visiting; she had enough on her plate with her husband Max, two small children and Mother's intermittent 'escapes' from Pop. I was happy making my own way in life. I continued to see Monica and Hilary and visited Sheelagh who'd married Barry and given birth to Kerry, my godson. I holidayed with them in Guernsey when they were on home leave from Kenya and exercised my cycling legs by cycling round the island with Barry.

I attended St Ebbes Anglican Church in Oxford which was evangelical and filled with Christian students every Sunday who sat and took notes with enthusiasm during Reverend Weston's sermons. Perhaps unintentionally, the vicar's wife and other parishioners overlooked me several times when they invited my colleagues to their homes. In my hurt, I began to withdraw rather than assert my presence. As a church they have resolutely rejected women's ordination which, given the later events of my life, now makes me smile. In 1965 I was pleased to reconnect with the young woman who had invited me to the youth group at Nairobi Cathedral after my father's death in 1960. She had married a curate and was briefly at St Aldgate's Church in the centre of Oxford.

Every girl in Oxford yearned to go to a college May Ball – except me. Other nurses from my set seemed to take pity on me when they pestered me.

'We're all going to the Baliol May Ball. Come with us, Audrey, we'll find you a partner.'

As I realised later, their motives were mixed. There was an army paramedic training in the Emergency Department who wanted to come, and I was the bunny being asked to partner him. I felt uncomfortable with the whole idea, but I wanted to experience an Oxford Ball. I put on finery and off we went, and my date proved as I thought, not at all interested in me. As it turned out he didn't appeal to me either so we soon lost one another. This left me milling around trying to look as though I was enjoying myself, but feeling like a fish out of water. One of Gilly's postgraduate beaux, Tudor, kindly rescued me and sought to engage me in a debate about Christianity as we queued for supper. He was too bright for me. I felt inadequate and that he wasn't really interested in my muddled thoughts as we discussed Christianity. After supper we wandered off in separate directions. Later in life, Tudor made a name for himself as an adventurer and author and converted to Judaism. The whole evening was an interesting experience but one I was happy not to repeat. I breathed a sigh of relief as I climbed my ladder and shut the trap door on it all.

Meanwhile back at the Radcliffe, I was in my third year with a much easier cap to fold and more responsibility. Throughout my training I spent very little time in the main theatres and in the Emergency Department. My time in theatre was mostly spent transporting radium in lead boxes or running around. I had difficulty hearing what was being said because of the masks and head scarves people wore. I was poorly taught in theatre practices and felt very inadequate and anxious. As a result, I only learned to dislike theatre and I very nearly gave up my chosen career at that point. I was dissuaded by my Aunt Hilda and Uncle George who were managing an aged-care hostel in Woodstock at the time. Hilda was my Father's younger sister. I could have enjoyed my time in Emergency if it had been longer.

During this third year I returned to the Churchill Hospital, where I had begun my training, and spent three months on the adult and children's plastic surgery wards. I hoped to be posted there for my staffing year as it was fascinating work, made more interesting by the plastic surgeon's scarlet trouser braces. The work varied from children having their protruding ears pinned back, to the treatment of a severely burned eight-year-old who had kicked an old oil drum onto a farm bonfire only to have it explode. I learnt to love the care of children in this ward. The adult wards covered procedures from surgery to enlarge or reduce women's breasts to the closure of a protruding meningocele – the sac containing the spinal cord – in an adult with spina bifida. I didn't get to be a staff nurse on a plastics ward. Instead, I completed my final months of training on Morris Ward, a women's medical ward at the Radcliffe and remaining there as a staff nurse.

Being given responsibility for a ward began early in our training, usually on night duty. There were about 30 beds in a ward, and they were often full. The routines and procedures typically kept the care flowing along, and the learning curves came with the unexpected events; the sudden admissions, emergencies, staffing issues or distressed relatives. Escorting the Registrar on ward rounds meant knowing your patients by name, diagnosis, treatment and current issues. Often the nurse knew more than the medical students who trailed behind the Registrar. In Oxford, there was a good relationship between medical students and nurses (in more ways than one for some), and a few medical students would visit the wards to learn dressing techniques from us. One Nigerian houseman would tease me: 'I'm the witch doctor,' alluding to my colonial past and chipping away at my worldview and lingering childhood prejudices. I liked him.

When the medical students had British Medical Association final examinations, nurses would be asked to chaperone the voluntary patients. The patient I chaperoned had a prolapsed uterus, and after several questions the 'almost doctor' was puzzled. I stood there deliberately looking at him, giving little coughs until he twigged that this was the test he'd omitted. I hoped it was only nerves that caused his lapse and he became a competent doctor.

Nerves hit me during my final practical exam. I was faced with a room full of items placed there to help me demonstrate a technique, a bench displaying theatre instruments I needed to identify and then I would need to answer situational questions. Halfway through I felt faint; I must have been holding my breath.

'I'm feeling faint, may I sit down sister?' I sat in a chair.

'Are you unwell Nurse Payne?' she said with concern.

'No, this happens sometimes, I'm sorry. What happens now?'

'If you leave now you will be marked on what you have done to this point.' I tried to get up and felt faint again.

'Sit here for a while, and I'll ask sister to come and speak with you.' I was near tears. I knew I needed to do more to be sure of a pass. Another examiner settled on the next chair and began to ask me questions about obstetrics and gynaecology. I relaxed and cheerfully answered them all. What a relief and how kind! We all went to the pub to celebrate the end of exams and then came the long wait for our results. A month later the mail brought good news in a thin brown envelope and I become a State Registered Nurse. In another six months the world became my oyster. I was no pearl, but I had grit. It would take more layers of life for me to gain any sense of inner value.

Reflection

My feelings surprised me as I recalled these years. I felt sick with anxiety in parts, and understood – perhaps for the first time – just how I felt for much of my time in certain areas of nursing. I know I was a good hospital nurse, but I'm pleased I found my niche later within community health. Nursing opened doors to so many places and specialities, and this is what suited my enquiring nature. It is also one way to, 'Love your neighbour as yourself.' Matthew 22:38

Seven

RETURN TO KENYA

Trees sparkle with ripe raindrops;
trout swim upstream to favourite spots.
Watery sunshine lights a pool
as morning mists meet daytime cool.
*

We pick our flies,
choose the ties,
flex our rods and whip the air.
Whoosh! flick, flick, wading in,
it's icy cold as we begin.
Whoosh! Flick! I do the same
…. line gets snagged and hangs in shame.
*

The Catch of the Day swims right by;
watching it pass, I wonder why,
it waves a fin in mock salute
and signals others to follow suit.

The highlands of Kenya with its mix of farms, forests, townships and villages lies 6500 feet (1981m) above sea level and 300km north-west of Nairobi. The shrinking world of my teenage years is expanding once more as I breathe in the crisp morning air of Africa. I'm in Kaptagat and realising trout fishing is a skill I may not want to pursue further. All forms of hunting disturb me; I prefer animals to be alive and well, despite my carnivorous diet. East Africa was considered the birthplace of prehistoric mankind, but any vestiges of the ancient hunter-gatherer in me fell off me eons ago.

A conversation with a visiting Kenyan in 2017 triggered memories of my return to Kenya in 1967. I asked Archdeacon Sammy, 'How big is Kaptagat now?'

'Ah, let me see; about 40,000 people.' He smiled at the surprise on my face. This meant 65 square kilometres of land was supporting a large population. Perhaps it wasn't so surprising given that it was 50 years since I'd made that first return to the country of my childhood. I told Sammy a little of my connection with his home district and discovered that Kaptagat Preparatory School where I had worked, was still thriving. My mind returned to my return to Kenya in 1967 when I first viewed it with adult eyes.

It began with an advertisement I spotted in *The Daily Telegraph's* Situations Vacant column.

'Look at this, Gilly!' I thrust the paper under the nose of my flat mate and good friend. 'It's for a school nurse in Kenya!' Excitement thrilled through me at this unexpected opportunity to get back to the country that had been home.

'Will you apply?'

'Oh yes, but I expect I'll be up against lots of others.' I was quite convinced that every nurse in the world would be jumping at this job. My heart was pounding as I wrote a carefully worded application and thumped even harder when I read the response days later. 'Please come for an interview in London,' it said.

I arrived at the given address in good time and Mrs Chitty, the school principal's wife, made me welcome. We drank coffee as we talked, and about

20 minutes later she said she had another candidate to see and would let me know. The next day she phoned to say the position was mine. I was so excited. I was to become Sister Audrey, which was a bonus after three years of wearing a badge emblazoned with the encouraging statement, *Nurse A Payne*. I went to tell Matron Biddulph I was leaving, knowing I'd only completed half the required year as a staff nurse. I wondered if I'd get a hostile reception, but this matron was not of Miss Preddy's ilk and had nursed in Kenya herself. She understood; 'You want to get home, Audrey?'

'Yes, please, but will I still be able to have my hospital badge?'

'I think we can arrange that.'

I wore my bronze Nurses Guild badge with pride until it was stolen many years later. Miss Biddulph and I corresponded for some years; she liked to hear about Kenya.

I flew out of Gatwick Airport after spending the day with Bill and Dorothy Beck, grandparents of my schoolfriend, Sheelagh. They had moved from the Kenya coast to Haywards Heath in Surrey, and it was good to reconnect with them. They waved me off as I boarded the train to Gatwick Airport, little knowing that our next meeting would be in Australia. My flight landed in Rome and Khartoum before descending at Entebbe. The emotions that rose at first sight of East Africa's red earth took me by surprise. I choked back tears as memories and nostalgia fought for dominance. The long-imagined smell of Africa's earth reached me before we landed. The plane's approach path took us over clusters of round thatched huts, then over the lake's blue water with its swirling eddies and languishing canoes. We bounced onto terra firma and taxied to a halt within walking distance of the white control tower and passenger terminal. I paused in surprise as I entered the transit lounge. There was our family friend Noel who'd managed to persuade the officials to allow him into that restricted area to greet me. Noel, with his studious glasses and wicked north country sense of humour, had lived as a paying guest with our family in Nairobi when I was a child. We had an hour to catch up. He'd married his Irish girlfriend Maisie, produced three children and had become manager of the Standard Bank in Kampala.

A year later I spent a strange two weeks of joy and anxiety with him and Maisie. We visited game parks, and I met some very kind people. Sadly, I offended Maisie by taking liberties with her sewing machine to mend something and became the butt of her Irish temper. It was deserved, but I reeled from her verbal beating. Maisie knew nothing of my life experience with Pop's drunken anger and violence, or she may have curbed some of it. In the event, her outburst numbed me for days, and the rift remained – something I have always regretted. It taught me to tread more carefully as a guest and as a single woman in a world of twosomes.

I was more nostalgic than tearful as we flew over Nairobi Game Park to land at Embakasi Airport. Mrs Chitty met me and we drove to Kaptagat that day. It was a five-hour trip through Kikuya lands and down the winding escarpment road into the basin of the Great Rift Valley. Little stalls selling uncured sheepskins, colourfully woven baskets and wooden carvings were set up along the roadside. In later years, cautionary billboards grew up along this roadside. My favourite was; '*Haraka haraka, haina baraka*.' translating as, 'Hasten, hasten, has no blessing'. Our closest equivalent is probably, 'More haste less speed.'

That return journey was full of nostalgia and flashes of the past. It felt surreal; familiar yet different. We drove past the thorn trees and giraffe around Naivasha, seeing the pink hue of the lake caused by algae that attracted seasonal gatherings of thousands of flamingos. As we climbed to higher altitudes, tea plantations came onto the landscape with their distant swathes of bright green against the blue sky. The air temperature dropped. We turned off the bitumen road before the small town of Eldoret and headed to Kaptagat on a rough dirt road that became very familiar to me on my weekly trips into the shops and social activities of Eldoret.

The air thinned and the landscape became a mix of shrub, farmland and villages. We banged our open hands on the outside of our car doors, to hurry along the cattle being herded on the road by young boys, 'Shoo! Shoo!' Half an hour later, dusty and tired, we drove into the school's driveway, bounced over several speed humps, and came to a halt on the edge of a cluster of buildings set around a large sports field. We'd arrived at what would be my workplace for the next two years. The journey brought us from Nairobi's altitude of 5600 feet to Kaptagat's 6800 feet, and I was beginning to feel the difference. A high-altitude sports training facility was built in later years not far from Kaptagat forest at Iten, where the altitude is 8000 feet (2400m). The altitude slowed and tired me during those first weeks of adjustment. Kaptagat was cold enough for a log fire at night and the sun was deceptively fierce with the equator only 58km (36 miles) away.

Kaptagat Prep School was a private primary school. Before Kenya's independence in 1963, this part of the country was known as 'the White Highlands' due to its mainly British settlers who had established large pro-ductive farms. In 1967 some of the old settler families still lived in the region, taking Kenyan citizenship in order to hang onto their farms and disappearing lifestyle. Life had become uncertain under President Jomo Kenyatta's policy of returning land to African ownership.

I became good friends with brothers Francis and Robert Foster, who had once owned the land on which the school was built. As bachelors approach-ing middle-age, they shared the responsibilities of their farm and enjoyed other pastimes like hunting, shooting, fishing and playing polo. Their fre-quent long weekends stretched from Thursday to Tuesday, and I teased them by calling Wednesday their working week. Francis organised the farm work while the older Robert would sit on the farmhouse verandah paying only those bills stamped with 'Final Demand'. The paid invoices would go into his unique filing method, which was essentially a scattered mess on the floor. He did this mainly to aggravate red-haired Francis. Robert was the mechanic, and their pet hornbill would run off with nuts and bolts from whatever engine he was repairing. The farmhouse furniture was covered in animal skins, mostly shot years before by their parents. In the evening, a wood fire was lit in the stone grate and supper was an intimate, infor-mal affair. The beautifully maintained garden sloped down to a stream that ran alongside green lawns and blossoming herbaceous borders. Bugs, small beasts and the odd snake lurked in the undergrowth. I was enchanted by it all and over time felt very at home there.

Both brothers were good company, amusing, kind and generous. I first dated one, then the other, wondering what marriage would be like in their household. But each undermined the other's romances, possibly out of concern that it would be too big a change to their unique, established patterns of life. I'm grateful for all the friendship and new experiences they gave me. It was what I needed after the past seven years. They gave me a glimpse into a very different way of life, full of eccentricities and strong, kind characters. I enjoyed wonderful anecdotes about their parents and grandparents' days and their exploits in the bush and during their Kenya Regiment days. In those years at Kaptagat I learnt to fly fish, unsuccessfully; to shoot on a rifle range, successfully, and drive proficiently on dirt roads in all weather and conditions.

Kaptagat school attracted about 100 pupils aged between six and twelve from various cultural and racial backgrounds. I prided myself on remembering each child's name, and the 'San' (sanitorium) became a haven for some of the very young and homesick ones. The youngest was a five-year-old boy who was still learning to socialise with other children, having spent all his young life on an isolated farm speaking Nandi or Luo languages to farm children. There were Ugandan politicians' children who would return from school holidays with tales of tanks rolling along the streets of Kampala and attempted coups. At the start of the school terms, a few Ugandans would not return; such were the politics of the day.

One Ugandan student was Richard Walugembe. He was a son of the *kubaka* (king) of Buganda who lived in exile in England, having been deposed as the first President of Uganda in 1966. Richard was his fifth and favourite son (so I was told) and he was a tall, good-looking boy with an infectious sense of humour. He was a good rugby player in a somewhat flamboyant way that made him play to the spectators more than the ball. One morning as he was listening to his little transistor radio under his pillow, he heard news of his father's death in London. It was a suspicious death and probably a murder, but that was never proven. It was a devastating way for anyone to learn of their father's death.

My stepfather died unexpectedly around this time, although in less dramatic circumstances. I received the news by letter some three weeks after his death and wished I'd known earlier. I can't say I mourned him, but I pondered on what I knew of his life and felt a great sadness when I first heard. He was not a happy man, but in good times he was very kind to me.

I enjoyed all the school's children at Kaptagat, and was given the dubious privilege of giving individual swimming lessons to those who were fearful in the school's swimming pool. Weekend entertainment could be a film when the children became more distressed about hurt animals, especially horses, than the killing of 'goodies or baddies'. They loved animals, and so did I, even if the furry ones gave me hay fever.

One morning the children pointed out of the clinic doorway. 'Look, Sister Audrey, Emma's brought her little ones.'

Emma was the farm's huge, proud sow and she took every litter on a guided tour of the school grounds. We all enjoyed seeing her lead her line of six or seven piglets with a proprietary air passing the classrooms. Then (sad silence), one school evening meal-time caused me to forswear pork.

'This is lovely meat, a nice change from mutton,' said one staff member and we all agreed.

'Yes, this is Emma.'

I choked in my dismay and refused the offer of crackling. Any pig meat was approached with caution because they carry tapeworm, but after that meal I became my own version of kosha. Perhaps I wouldn't have made a good farmer's wife after all.

Our days were marked out by school activities and each evening we would wait for the chugging of the school's generator starting before the lights came on. Anyone within earshot of the generator housing could learn some innovative Punjabi swear words as Mr Singh battled with the old motor or caught yet another finger in the machinery. I made 9.45pm my bedtime in readiness for the generator to be turned off at 10pm. This habit was reinforced years later in Papua New Guinea and remained with me, even in the city. Mr Singh's loss of fingers upset the school's cook for all the wrong reasons. He once complained to me during an attendance for his recurrent chest infection – 'It's not right Sister, Mr Singh got money for his lost fingers, and I get nothing because I have a bad chest.'

I failed to find a satisfactory answer.

In Eldoret, I became friends with several Afrikaners through my hairdresser who was married to one, and my contacts at the rifle club. I had joined the club because it was the only activity on a Thursday afternoon, my half day off. I knew very little about the South Africans' historical connection with Eldoret.

'When did you come to Kenya?' I asked my new friends.

'Our families came up with the Trek,' they said, expecting me to know what that was. I imagined 'Wild West' wagons loaded with families and goods rattling up bush tracks from South Africa in the early 1900s. This would have taken months, maybe years of hard travelling and living, and I admired such pioneering spirit and stamina. I wondered why my friends' families trekked so far in those early years. Legend has it that Maasai herdsmen spotted ox wagons carrying the first Afrikaner settlers to the land around Eldoret in 1906. About 700 Boers known as the 'irreconcilables' were the first to arrive. These were Afrikaners who'd supported the British in South Africa's Boer War. This presumably made them persona-non-grata with the other Boers, leading to their migration. An additional 100 people arrived by ox cart in 1911, and the population increased so that by the 1940s, a community of several thousand Afrikaners farmed 1000 square miles of Kenyan land. Its market centre became Eldoret, which supported three Dutch Reformed churches. Only a handful of Afrikaner families remained after Kenya's independence in 1963, and I expect those I met in 1968 have long since left. I visited one of the Afrikaner farms with a friend and was fascinated by their housing arrangement of individual *rondavals* (mud and wattle huts) as bedrooms, a central family area and outside kitchen. I had expected a more European or Dutch experience.

I was assisted in the school sanitorium by an able young local man, James. His limp was due to childhood polio, and in better circumstances he would have made a good nurse. On the day Neil Armstrong landed on the moon, I took James outside and pointing upwards, told him in my inadequate Swahili: 'Look up, James. A man is walking on the moon right now!'

'*Hapana*, Sister' (No).

'*Kweli.*' (Truly). And I had no way to prove it to him or explain further.

'*Hapana!*' he said, grinning in disbelief. He probably laughed with his friends telling them how Sister played a joke on him. Oh well, I tried.

During this time, I renewed my connection with Sheelagh and Barry and their two small sons, Kerry and Eric. They lived on a farm at Thika until they migrated to Western Australia in 1968. Sheelagh's parents, Frank and Doreen, lived and worked in Nairobi and again opened their home to me. How blessed I have been by the kindness of others. Doreen sold me her pale blue Triumph Herald at a minimal price. It proved to be a very nippy little car with front-wheel drive and particularly good on the muddy roads in the wet seasons. I spent Christmas holidays at the coastal township of Malindi with Frank, Doreen and their son Rodney who was about to start university in South Africa. Rodney's girlfriend Dee joined us, which led to my being their chaperone for a few days. Years later Rod and Dee told me that I wasn't a very efficient one.

An illness hit me during my second year at Kaptagat. It was probably pneumonia and relapsing malaria. I ended up in the hospital and took some weeks to recover before returning to work.

'You look different, Aunt Pad,' one of the Upson twins announced, using my nickname, the origins of which were obscure.

'I expect it's because I've lost some weight.' I'd also lost energy and was looking forward to school holidays. My illness unsettled me, and I began to consider a job offer in Mombasa. Kaptagat school was a good beginning for me as a newly qualified nurse and had brought me back to Kenya. But I disliked having half a day off each week and I missed hospital work. I'd inherited the restlessness that inhabited my father and after two years was ready to move. Some of my childhood memories had become reconciled with a more mature view of the realities of life in Kenya. It was time to face the Kenya coast and lay to rest the nostalgia I felt for childhood holidays.

Mombasa – my favourite place

I began work in Mombasa at the Katherine Bibby Hospital, which prior to 1964 had been known as the European Hospital. By 1970 the hospital had become a private inter-racial hospital with about 60 beds. As a ten-year-old I'd spent a miserable week in the isolation room of its children's ward, being treated for a gastric bug or malaria, or both. The year after I began work at the Katherine Bibby, my niece Faye was in that same ward with a similar complaint. How I felt for her lying in that glassed-in isolation ward!

Mombasa was where I felt most at home, although not always at ease because of Kenya's political landscape. On my return, the Kenyan antagonism towards expatriates was part of the adjustment to *Uhuru* (freedom). The slightest mistake or infringement by a foreigner would bring instant deportation. Despite this, Mombasa gave me a sense of wellbeing and place that I'd not experienced since leaving Africa. It felt like my natural habitat with its monsoonal climate, its broad white beaches to the north and south and its protective coral reef. It was tropical, beautiful and exciting; the best ingredients for the recipe of my life at that time.

A Potted History

Part of Mombasa's attraction was its Arabic features and history. The truth about Mombasa is that its beauty was only skin deep. Digging deeper lays bare its entanglement in the ancient East African trading routes that became part of the slave trade. Mombasa Island was one of the many old Swahili-Arab coastal settlements that existed along Africa's eastern coastline between

Mogadishu in Somalia and the Zambezi River in Mozambique. These places offered safe harbour for rapacious Arab traders who travelled from the Arabian Gulf countries up and down the coast on the Indian Ocean's trade winds. Trade in many goods reached inland as far as the lower Nile, but the slave trade grew as the Western world's demand for slave labour increased. In the 19th century, as many as 50,000 slaves passed annually through nearby Zanzibar's slave markets, many of whom would have come through Mombasa.

Perched on the cliffs overlooking the old harbour was the Katherine Bibby Hospital where I worked from 1970-72. Not far along these same cliffs the Portuguese had built and named Fort Jesus whose thick stone walls guarded the entrance to Mombasa's old harbour. The Portuguese came to this part of East Africa in the 1400s and ruled for a couple of centuries until it was taken back by the Omani Sultanate of Zanzibar in the 1600s. The British Empire established the East Africa Protectorate in 1895 and from 1920 it became known as the Kenya Colony.

The village close to where my parents bought land in the 1950s had an oral history that recalled the name of the explorer and missionary David Livingstone. Perhaps one of their number had been a bearer or interpreter for him all those years before. Livingstone was known to have recruited coastal Swahili people.

The late Miss Case, my high school history teacher, might have been pleased to know how much I remember of all that she taught us about East African history.

The People

In the early 1970s, Mombasa's society had a richer mix of cultures than upcountry Kenya because of its coastal location with large docks and tourism. The coast continued to be as Arabic as it was Swahili (the coastal tribe), although it hosted fewer Arabs travelling the trade wind routes and accommodated more people from inland tribes. At night we nurses stood on the verandah of the Katherine Bibby Hospital to watch the wooden dhows glide ghostlike into the old harbour by moonlight, silent except for the weather-worn creaking of their rigging and lateen sail. The end of our night shift was also Arabic and heralded by the imam's call to prayer from the local mosque. His voice would echo out across the silence as the morning light filtered into the wards and the noises of the morning would start. Sometimes it appeared that even the birds waited for that call before they began their dawn chatter.

The meld of cultures at the coast appealed to the senses and fascinated the curious such as me. It was Africa, yet the streets bustled with European shoppers, Indian traders and African markets – people who lived juxtaposed lives yet remained separate socially. My parents taught us to respect other cultures and we had to wear a dress or jeans in town. I continued to do this when I returned as an adult. Yet we remained within our worldview of superiority and paternalism and this took me more years to overcome.

Shopping in the new and old parts of town immersed me in the scents of jasmine, orange water and cloves, all co-mingled with the aroma of garam masala and meals being cooked in back kitchens. Shops displayed open sacks of spices, bright orange turmeric and yellow saffron; trays presented bright red chilli peppers and bundles of coriander. However, as though to dispel any rising romantic notions, the reality of poor plumbing and open drains would intrude and the gutters of the narrow back streets bred rubbish, flies and mosquitos. Dogs and children played in these streets, and the sounds of laughter, arguments and bartering articulated the hustle and bustle of life to a background of multilingual music tastes. At night fierce looking Arabs, complete with scimitars on their belts, would sit in twos and threes under the main street lights, playing cards and unknown games, and maybe negotiating a return cargo for their dhows. There were Arab-styled coffee urns and small cups placed between them. Away from the bazaar, the contrasting nightlife of upmarket tourism hotels and clubs witnessed dinner dances, and nightclubs, dives and brothels occupied visiting sailors and other adventurers.

Mombasa bazaar was where I had my ears pierced for ten shillings including the sleepers, with no resultant infection. In a small side street café, I ate delicious Indian curries with a boyfriend, with no ill effects from either.

But I had my first hangover after an evening meal at a smart hotel with the same boyfriend. I only realised what had caused my headache the next day when I bumped into a friend who'd been with us the previous evening:

'I have a thumping headache, and I can't think why,' I said in all innocence, peering out of my dark glasses. The friend laughed and gave me a wise look. The penny dropped. *Never again,* I thought, feeling rather foolish. The boyfriend in question was a heavy drinker, and my later engagement to him lasted a week. Without the experience of my stepfather's alcoholism, I may have made a disastrous marriage and had more serious headaches.

Indians and Pakistanis were early migrants to Kenya, having been imported as labourers by the British. The women would shimmer with their traditional dress, dhoti pants and flowing saris. An Indian nursing friend would bring her modern saris to work, mostly during night duty. Some had appliqued designs, others were low on the hip, and I would try them on when there was a lull in the ward's activity. Europeans could be as fascinatingly different as other groups, bringing their cultures from different parts of Europe. I became friends with Errol, the English wife of a taciturn Polish architect, Sbish. She patiently taught me to water ski on Tudor Creek's shark-infested waters. It still took me two weeks to stand on my skis. Errol became a well-known author, writing about Kenya's past. The British, of course, came with more than their fair share of eccentricities and social misfits. Perhaps I was such a one.

Glimpsing the daily activities of other cultures and wondering about their lives and beliefs failed to shift my ethnocentricity or challenge my ambivalence about commitment to an inherited Christian faith. I explored Islam briefly, discarded Hinduism, looked at Buddhism and remained an agnostic. My beliefs clarified over time, but my ability to communicate across cultures was born in Africa and especially in Mombasa.

In all, Mombasa was a dreamer's delight and a public health nightmare, a mingling of mystique and muck. It was also a place in which to fall in love, which I did several times.

Aspects of my life had been in hibernation since 1960, and I blossomed in Mombasa in my mid-20s. Subconsciously, I was making up for lost teenage years. I enjoyed days off on the beach and being invited to dinner and dances by young men. When expatriates on two-year contracts asked where I came from, I enjoyed saying firmly, 'Here. I grew up here.'

My school friend, Joan, was the hospital physiotherapist when I began working at the Katherine Bibby Hospital. Working with Joan was a bonus. We'd been in the same year and boarding house at the Kenya High School, and I'd spent some happy school holidays with her at her home in Nyali, on the mainland of Mombasa. She became like a sister to me. Joan was an only child, and when she married and moved to work in Thailand I became her mother's surrogate daughter, helping to fill the gap Joan left. This open home was a great gift to me, and Joan's mother Muriel became a firm friend. Her father was always kind but was somewhat scary as an 'alpha male' that demanded due deference and respect. He'd lived in Malaya as a child and had bouts of dysentery that made him very grouchy.

In the nurses' quarters, known militarily as the Sisters Mess, I had a spacious room with a verandah that overlooked the old harbour. Air-conditioning was the sea breeze and a fan. All meals were provided and tea or orange juice was brought to our rooms each morning. Yet again, I didn't have to expand my basic cooking knowledge. The nurses' mess had inherited a small thatched cottage near Diani, one of Mombasa's southern beaches. We could book this and two or three of us would go there for our nights off. There was a small family hotel nearby, but it wasn't a usual tourist spot, so we had most of the beach to ourselves. We swam, relaxed and ate local lobsters bought for a pittance from a local fisherman. At night we'd light the Tilly pressure lamps and read, lying on our beds under the mosquito nets. I thought I was in heaven, except on the day I was stung by a Portuguese man o' war jellyfish. The pain was excruciating, but it eventually subsided.

Mombasa's modern, busy port has been long re-established on the other side of the island and visiting ship's crew often phoned the hospital to invite nurses out – any would do. I felt quite affronted by this, complaining that we weren't an escort agency and refused all invitations on principle. Sometimes I would go on board with Joan's parents or friends who worked in shipping. Eventually, I succumbed to the Royal Navy officer's cocktail parties and developed a few friendships along the way. I became friends with Zena and Bill, a gregarious New Zealand couple I met through a colleague. We all enjoyed dancing and they would invite me to local discos to make up numbers. This was a safer way to be out at night, and it kept me very fit. I began to make my own clothes using the boldly designed local fabrics, and occasionally splashing out to buy the latest smart 'hot pants' or trouser suit. The fashions of the 1970s were fun for the young. Years later, when I threw out my six pairs of old bikinis, I wondered how I ever fitted into them. A sad day!

Hospital work

The work was varied on the upstairs general wards and it fluctuated in intensity. We cared for a mix of patients, including local residents, tourists, sailors and men, women and children. Some shipping lines were notorious for their poor on-board living conditions and when they were in port there would be more sailors admitted. The doctors were mostly wise to the malingerers, but some were excellent actors and played out complex symptoms that would cause them to be repatriated to their homeland. We nursed Greek, Japanese, Chinese, Dutch and Africans, all with different languages, diets and faiths. Then there were tourists and expatriate residents of all ages presenting with traumatic injuries, medical and surgical conditions and tropical diseases. In the nurses' office was a list of useful phrases in various languages. The one that proved to be universally understood was 'piss!'

Life on the wards in Mombasa could be many things – heart-warming, sad, amusing and even mysterious: an apparently-well sailor willed himself to die because a relative said a curse had been placed on him. The experienced doctor said he'd seen this happen before and whatever caused him to die remained a puzzle.

We also laughed a lot and some happenings amused us for weeks. One such event was the time when thirsty elephants some 50km away broke the main water pipe into Mombasa. They'd stomped on one of the weaker junctions to get at the water. The local fire brigade delivered water to essential services that week and the hospital water tank was on the flat roof outside the men's ward. Firemen climbed up ladders onto the roof holding the nozzle end of the hose, while their colleagues at ground level blindly turned on the water at high pressure. Disaster struck. The large heavy tube escaped from the firemen on the roof and developing a will of its own, snaked across the rooftop.

'*Sidia*! Look out!'

The swollen grey canvas snake writhed around the roof rearing its nozzle into the air like an attacking cobra. The firemen ran around the roof yelling at this seemingly alive thing and tried in vain to catch it. The lively hose dodged the men, performed several magnificent fly-pasts before rearing up its nozzle outside the ward's open window. It joyfully soaked six unsuspecting Chinese patients, who were sitting up in their beds watching proceedings with interest.

'Ooo! – ahh! – water in! water in! Sister!' went up the cry. We were so busy laughing it was difficult to sympathise.

Tourists arrived as patients after road crashes or other encounters. Many people who were only used to seeing animals in zoos were inclined to ignore the game park signs telling them to stay in their cars. We admitted one Greek man who had jumped out of his tour car in Tsavo Park to get closer to the elephants. One charged and he slipped. The elephant's tusk pierced his groin causing severe blood-loss and significant injuries. He was lucky to survive and was eventually flown to Spain, where there were experts in goring injuries that occurred in bull fighting.

Mombasa was also a recreational port for American GIs serving in Vietnam. Their recreation sometimes caused their hospitalisation. We learned to be very cautious about taking their night time observations of pulse, respiration, blood pressure.

'If you wake me up tonight, I'll attack you,' one warned me.

'Why?' I ask naively.

'I'll think you're Viet Cong.'

Not one patient was lost for lack of their night time nursing observations. If they were breathing, we left them alone. That distant war, killing and twisting the bodies and minds of so many, became more real to me through these very young men. However, in a different sense we did lose four patients one evening. The police found them some hours later at a local nightclub where they were happily playing in the band, still in their hospital pyjamas. This and other tales would possibly fill another book, but these few antics provide a taste of the good memories.

During this time Frances and Max with their daughters Clare and Faye also came to work and live in Mombasa. I had initiated their move to Nairobi by letting them know of an opening for a chef at the Muthaiga Club. They then moved to Mombasa where Max worked at the airport overseeing airline catering. It was a treat to have them living nearby and it made me feel even more 'local' rather than an expatriate. However, Max suffered a head injury from an accident on his motor scooter and was admitted to the Katherine Bibby Hospital before being transferred to Nairobi for surgery. Once recovered, he worked in a small Mombasa hotel briefly and then returned to England. Perhaps his brush with death made him think more seriously about God; he became a committed Christian through a German chef who was visiting the port with the Christian mission ship, *Logos*. This left me as the sole agnostic of my immediate family.

Then I fell in love with a Scottish doctor and had an interesting and happy year of knowing him and meeting many interesting people through him. I still smile when I remember those days. It took time for me to fully realise that he was not going to commit to a more permanent relationship, even after he'd returned to England to study psychiatry. I'd decided to follow him and so my time in Kenya closed.

Flying out of Nairobi I looked out of the window at the receding Ngong Hills and told myself, 'I'll return,' but I knew Kenya would never be a true home for me again. I leaned back in my seat and wondered, *What next?*

Reflection

I have enjoyed reliving this period of my life as little details popped into my mind, reminding me of people, places and small adventures. I see my maturation and understand my need for that return to the country of my childhood. It reconnected the flailing emotions of my unwanted first departure, healed some of the raw edges and gave me some perspective.

My spirituality appeared to be dormant in those years, but I had a disturbing dream while I was in Mombasa. I was in the bazaar when a flood came, and I swam frantically towards a dinghy holding three people. 'Help me in!' I cried. 'No,' they called back, 'you've had your chance, and we're not saving you again.' And I woke up. Make of this what you will, but I thought I'd been locked out of salvation. I should have turned to the story of the prodigal son in Luke 15.

Eight

Interlude

Interlude, the space between
what is now,
what has been,
moving on.
*

Hurting heart,
muddled head,
feeling blue,
little said,
moving on.
*

Interlude, a space between
a resting point,
a change of scene,
and moving on.

My 29th birthday coincided with a leap year, a time in our cultural calendar when women may propose to men. This was a step too far for me, and I knew my beau too well to expect him to commit to marriage. Perhaps if I'd proposed, I'd have been forced to face reality, and the inevitable unravelling of our love affair would have been less painfully extended. Love wears blinkers.

Elsewhere that year, Nixon's presidency was under pressure from the Watergate tape disclosures and the toll of the Vietnam War. In Europe, the Munich Olympic Games belatedly ramped up its security. The Palestinian terrorist group, Black September, took eleven Israeli athletes hostage and killed them. On a lighter note, it was also the year pop group ABBA was formed, and David Bowie stepped onto the stage as his alter ego, Ziggy Stardust. I wore maxi dresses, miniskirts, long boots and a PVC raincoat sporting large blue dots.

In Mombasa, President Jomo Kenyatta was wielding his ceremonial fly whisk and ordering all traffic to halt on the road verge whenever his cavalcade drove past. Kenya was flexing its political muscles. My love had returned to the UK and I was pining. I returned to a late English summer.

Skegness on the east coast of Lincolnshire was euphemistically called 'bracing' by British Rail. One sceptical friend joked that there wasn't much else to say about it, but it's where my mother chose to live after Pop died. It's a windy holiday town, full of holidaymakers known locally as 'trippers', eating candy floss in the summer. The locals battled umbrellas in the winter or went abroad. Mother's white bungalow was opposite the fifth tee of the local golf course, two miles from Gibraltar Point's Nature Reserve and Bird Observatory. She involved herself in local golf and church activities and seemed happy. Her sisters would visit, and she would go on golfing holidays with one or two of them. Frances and Max were able to stay on their return from Kenya, and their two daughters, Clare and Faye, spent a brief time at a local school.

It was here, as I was sitting on Mother's sofa with the usual afternoon cup of tea in hand, that I told her about falling in love in Mombasa and that I would consider living with him if he'd only ask. She heard me out, didn't moralise.

'Do think carefully about it, Audrey. You'll have people's disapproval to deal with, and it won't be easy.'

A fleeting sadness flickered across her face, causing me to wonder what she wasn't saying. The affair drifted, and I was left licking my heart wounds for the next 18 months. It seems that a healthy recovery from most of life's losses is about the same; two years of grief followed by a lifetime of memories. My nurse friend, Gilly, and her new husband, Richard, were very kind and let me stay with them in Guildford, south of London. I worked for several months at a nearby small private hospital, where the nuns tried to draw me into their faith and fold. I wasn't tempted. I have a treasured picture of blue irises painted by a favourite 91-year-old patient from that small hospital, given to me by her companion after her death.

The Surrey Nursing Agency knew I owned a current passport and asked me to escort an elderly lady to Portugal, where she kept a flat on the Algarve coast. I was vetted and approved by her son and advised to make sure she took her Valium tablets correctly and not to let her drive. The local housekeeper taught me to enjoy a roast sweet potato in place of a bread roll with my meals. Mrs Money, her real name, spent her days shopping and visiting friends, who were mostly expatriate retirees escaping the English weather and high cost of living. I'd drive her and was treated as 'below stairs' until the friends realised I'd grown up in Kenya, and somehow this made me more socially acceptable. I'll never understand the British social system. Mrs Money was quite the eccentric, and I stayed with her for several months, laughing a lot, enjoying her racy tales about her several marriages and hearing her insights on life among the more privileged of society. She told her stories so frankly and vividly that I'm sure her doctor visited at sundowner time mostly to hear more of her stories.

The Algarve coast was an embryonic tourist destination with several high-rise, expensive hotels beginning to spoil the views. Mrs Money knew the Portuguese owner of one, and we would be treated royally whenever we visited. She would flirt outrageously with him to ensure our free lunch. Then my determined charge decided to drive.

'You don't need to see the whites of their eyes to avoid them,' she declared, while peering through the windscreen with her failing eyesight. I'd hang onto the door handle as she narrowly missed another jaywalker.

An American couple Elli and Bill, who'd befriended me, heard that another expatriate needed a nurse and Mrs Money and I amicably parted company. Bill hinted that he and Elli had been involved in anti-Vietnam demonstrations, making them personae non gratae to their government. They could live cheaply in Portugal and wait out their time before returning home. I kept in touch with them for about ten years after they went back to their careers as social workers in England, then Massachusetts, USA.

My second patient was a delightful 80-year-old, tall English gentleman with mobility problems and early dementia. His wife, Anne, was 20 years younger and found it difficult to cope with his declining health, having been cosseted as a child by older brothers and then by her husband. She often had one too many after dinner. Michael was big-framed although not heavy, and occasionally he'd take a tumble. I'd go into his room and start to lift him, only to end up on the floor too and here we would sit on the carpet like a couple of children giggling. His prostate problems worsened, and to my surprise, he cheerfully accepted wearing a cumbersome 1970s urine bag. I wondered why.

'In the House of Lords, they all wear them,' he proclaimed with a grin.

Since that revelation, I've not viewed the ceremonial opening of Parliament without a smile.

During lunch, Michael would say: 'Well dear, I think I'll go into KL about four o'clock.' He'd been a rubber planter in Malaya. 'Of course, dear.' Anne had learnt to agree, knowing his decisions would soon be forgotten. During my time with Michael we did the rounds of the expatriate society, and their friends were more naturally accepting of me than Mrs Money's. Anne lent me their second car for my days off. It was a red Morris Mini Minor and I loved whizzing along in it to visit Elli and Bill. I only once found myself driving the wrong way around a roundabout as I adapted to driving on the other side of the road. Fortunately, the road was deserted at the time. After six weeks, I escorted Michael and Anne back to The London Clinic for his prostate surgery. Anne would phone me every few months, saying, 'Audrey, please come back. He calls every nurse we employ, Audrey.' I bet that irritated them.

⌁

My restlessness took me to London, where I rented a small bedsitter on the fourth floor of a house in Sussex Gardens, close to Hyde Park. I walked or caught the bus to a small college where I took a course in speed writing and typing, hoping this would broaden my job options. It didn't, but it was useful to have typing skills at 45 words a minute, and speed writing at 100 words a minute. The latter ruined my spelling but helped with taking lecture notes in years to come.

It was a strange two months that reaffirmed my decision that London in the 1970s, or any time, was not the place for me, despite some funny and enlightening incidents. I discovered the hard way that the previous occupant of my bedsitter had been a croupier at a smart club in the West End. She'd obviously diversified, because I continually received overseas calls from cultured voices with various accents. All asked when it would be convenient to call or make an appointment. Eventually, an Australian phoned who was more upfront.

'I suppose you don't do the same thing, do you?'

'No,' I laughed, 'but I'd have made a fortune by now if I did!'

Many years later I came back to a small hotel in Sussex Gardens with my husband; this felt seriously weird. My emotions were all over the place, trying to deal with past images and present delights.

Trees paraded their red and gold plumage, shimmied and shook it all off to stand naked before the approaching winter. I donned my boots and, like a child, kicked dead leaves on my daily walk. I was running out of savings, the course had ended and my lease was up. I went home to Mother in bracing Skegness, feeling very low in spirits. School friend, Sheelagh, had been encouraging me to visit Western Australia, where they'd settled on the south coast. Unexpectedly, Mother came to the rescue.

'Audrey, the winter's coming, and you're not happy. How about I pay your fare, and you visit Sheelagh?'

'Are you sure?' I'm amazed that she'd do this for me.

The cheapest fare was a flight to Singapore, then ship to Fremantle. I didn't like accepting her money but was thrilled by the thought of a new adventure. I wrote to Sheelagh, and she sent me the address of the local hospital. I applied for a job and booked my ticket. Life was looking brighter already. And that is how Mother finally let go of me to live my life, or that's how it felt to me at the time.

After a whirl of farewells, travel formalities and packing, I was on my way. It was the end of November, and my flight was crowded with Australians going home for Christmas. We landed in Singapore, were taken to a hotel overnight and then ferried to the MV *Patris*, to await departure in two days. Singapore law wouldn't let men with long hair into the city, and the young Australian men were busy cutting their hair, ready for either a trip into town or the approval of their mothers in Australia.

The MV *Patris* was previously the *Bloemfontein Castle* of the Union Castle Line and now part of the Greek Chandris Line. It was an old ship and rolled in choppy seas, but its layout was familiar to me as I'd travelled on Union Castle ships as a child. I shared a cabin with another girl, but saw very little of her. A young Englishman, Barry, befriended me and I was glad of his chaperoning as the returning Australians were drinking their way home.

A few days later, I was sitting on the deck, some way off Western Australia's flat coastline when a radio broadcast gave the results of the Australian Federal Election. The Labor Party was in, and Gough Whitlam was to be the new prime minister.

'This is the first time in 23 years that the Liberal/Country Party coalition has been defeated at the polls,' the announcer lilted.

Australia's Parliament was about to have a paradigm shift from centre-right to the socialist left. Some passengers raised a glass to Whitlam, while others went into glum huddles of consternation. This meant that on the 7th of December 1972, I entered a country with a changing political scene, none of which I understood. This scenario seemed somehow familiar, but more secure than my prior entry to Kenya.

Years later, as an Australian citizen, I was immensely pleased that my entry is now marked on Fremantle's Welcome Wall Stage 3, on panel number 473. The walls were part of the WA Museum's project marking Western Australia's 175th founding anniversary.

Fremantle Welcome Wall. The record of my arrival.

Australia

'Hands out in front with palms up, please,' the immigration official intoned. We docked in the port of Fremantle, 20km south of Perth city, and the official came aboard to screen us. We dutifully queued to stand before him as he looked up and down our forearms, turning our hands over and seeming to peer at our nails. The reason remained a mystery to me, and I knew better than to ask. *Is this for signs of disease, drugs, or neither?* I wondered. Whatever it was, I was cleared and joined another queue. There a man flicked through my passport, looked up with a smile and said, 'Welcome to Australia.' My British passport was stamped and, to my surprise, I became a temporary resident of Australia at the thump of a stamp. With the hindsight of years, it's likely that I ticked all the boxes of those times; young, British, single and a qualified nurse.

As I went down the gangplank into Customs Shed A, I was embarrassed by the sound of my shipboard acquaintance calling out, 'Audrey, don't get off!' The cry was taken up by others hanging over the ship's rails. My choice to disembark in Fremantle baffled the Eastern State Australians. Their view of the West was ingrained and derogatory. I waved and was relieved to be swept away by Barry, Sheelagh's husband, and their friend, John. My extra luggage couldn't be collected until the next day and we stayed overnight at John and his wife Cynthia's home in Rossmoyne, a suburb of Perth.

The unfenced gardens and manicured lawns were the first differences I noticed. Everywhere housing developments and shopping centres were being built or expanded. I felt an excitement run through me as I realised I was moving from an old, overcrowded world to a newly developing spacious one. As we drove through the countryside between Perth and Albany, I noted its barren dryness. It was December and mid-summer. It felt strange not to see people walking along the sides of the road. There was no sign of life, no wild animals, not even a kangaroo, only persistent flies at every stop.

Albany, Western Australia

I'd not expected to feel foreign or be culture shocked. I expected differences, but that the life and language would still be 'Anglo' and familiar

– how wrong I was. Over the coming weeks, these differences came in droves. I walked down the main street and was horrified at the mass of flies riding on people's backs. I was shocked to pass by a hotel's men-only bar and even more unimpressed by my footpath view of its utilitarian white-tiled walls. The monsoon-sized ditches on the roadsides were easy to accept, I'd seen them in Kenya. The English language used idioms and nuances of meaning that I misunderstood, and some things had different names; tarmac was bitumen, swimsuits were bathers, linen was manchester and Christmas crackers were bon-bons, and shops advertised 'specials' meaning a mark down in price. I needed to learn a new vocabulary. On the social scene 'bring a plate' meant bring something on it too; 'come for tea', meant come for the evening meal and 'come and watch the pennants' meant come to see a sports tournament, not visit the Roman Catholic church. And as for Aussie Rules Football… So, yes, I was culture shocked but I got over it. I still trip up from time to time. For all this, I knew that this was a place where I could live long-term. I liked the egalitarian nature of the people and the sense of a country going places. I woke to the sound of kookaburras laughing, and enjoyed the rugged coastline and unpopulated beaches and bays of the south coast. I also loved staying with Sheelagh and Barry and their two boys, being part of their lives for a month or two before Sheelagh helped me find a nearby house to rent. There were no flats or units in Albany at that time, only granny flats or converted, draughty verandahs.

The Nurses' Board of WA in Perth cleared me to work, and in January 1973 I began my first job in Australia at Albany Regional Hospital. I found the nursing protocols and techniques much the same as those in the UK and Kenya, and my training seemed to relate most closely to that of the Fremantle trained nurses. The pronunciation and names of some drugs were different, which confused me at times. Generally, this was because the emphasis was placed on another vowel so that Phen-er-gan became Phen-err-gan. Albany Regional Hospital was a government funded hospital with no resident doctors. Patients were treated by the local general practitioners. My first ward was the women's ward, and on my first shift I was advised not to let the other registered nurse have the drug cupboard keys, but not to let her know she was under suspicion of mismanagement. We also admitted more patients in one shift than I admitted ever again at this hospital. Every time I began a new job, something particularly challenging like this would happen on my first day.

I soon found my feet at work and began to make friends with other nurses. I enjoyed earning a good wage for a change, thanks to the Nurses Union that I was expected to join. I bought a Ford Taunus, my first venture into hire purchase and something my Father would have frowned on – 'If you can't afford it, don't buy it.' I was invited to social events with some of the other nurses and discovered Albany's 1970s 'swinging' culture was less swinging than London, but I still avoided it, just as I had in London. After one memorable evening when an unsavoury game was suggested, I asked my friend to take me home and decided it was time I widened my social options. I didn't fit and I felt safer driving myself to and from social gatherings, which is a habit that possibly began on that memorable evening.

Over the next eight months I came to see the potential of making Western Australia my home, but not Albany. It was a place to raise a family and I was a 30-year-old single woman within a married peer group. I moved to Perth and rented a unit in Claremont near the railway station, waking at six every morning when the first trains went through. I enjoyed the Perth climate and was happy working at Bethesda Private Hospital overlooking the Swan River. It reminded me of the Katherine Bibby Hospital in Mombasa, only there were no dhows or mosque calls.

I began midwifery training at King Edward Memorial Hospital in Perth the following year and re-learned that midwifery was not a favourite area of nursing. It was a joy to welcome newborn babies into the world, but that was all I could find to like about it. I undertook the training to complete the little knowledge I had from my general training in England. Also, I needed the certificate to work in rural areas and widen my nursing choices. I'd been a hospital-based ward nurse for ten years and I already disliked the Australian system of monthly rostered night duty and eight-hour night shifts. Mombasa spoilt me with better working conditions.

During my midwifery training I had a failed romance and became miserable and restless. I'd moved to share a unit with a nursing friend,

Carol-Anne, in the beach suburb of Cottesloe and enjoyed living in that area and sharing with Carol. With a midwifery certificate tucked under my belt, I began looking at my job options. I took it for granted that as a nurse I had many options. It's a versatile and rewarding career to choose.

Community Health Nursing

I heard of Community Health Nursing through a colleague, Jenny. This was a recently formed section of the Health Department of WA and an expansion of Public Health Nursing, similar to Health Visiting in the UK at that time. The Whitlam Government that had come into power as I sailed into Fremantle was throwing federal government funding at Aboriginal Health and this was a major focus of Community Health Services, especially in rural and remote areas. I applied for a field nurse position and was impressed by the friendly, approachable Director of Nursing, Mary Reid, who interviewed me. I recall the pink rose in the small vase on her desk and that she wasn't in a uniform.

The six-week orientation programme to the role was a mini-course in remote, rural nursing. We were taught to drive four-wheel-drive vehicles and the bare bones of additional nursing knowledge and skills. Our uniforms were turquoise culottes and blouse with tan cardigan and shoes, and a blue floppy hat for sun protection. We could be posted to any town or Aboriginal community in WA. The country north of Perth was still a mystery to me, and I was told I was posted to Derby, pronounced as it's spelt, not as for England's city of the same name. The north of the State was always short staffed during the monsoonal wet season. My background made it a predictable posting. I wanted another adventure and challenge, and I was about to have both these things and more.

Reflection

This year of fluctuating happiness and misery was caused as much by me as others. It showed I was not good at choosing men and made me make the unhealthy choice of guarding my heart in future. My adult experience had shown me poor male models: they leave one way or another (like Father), are at times abusive (like Pop) or let you down (as for Frances.) This was a year of changing places, and yet an interlude in my life journey. It took me from what had been, into a life that was to come. I gave no thought to God or my buried faith.

Nine

KIMBERLEY BEGINNINGS

Body screaming 'Let me sleep';
mind computing for the week.
Eyes closing,
brain composing,
pictures fading from my screen
dream
dream
dream

Waking up again in fright;
noises of the night:
fan rattling
leaves rustling
cockroach scuttling
gecko chuckling...

Moon shouting through the window,
marsh expands in silver glow,
'come and see a Dreamtime story,
see the Land in all its glory.'
Timeless, ancient, shafts of light
pierce my mind and quiet my soul.

Pictures changing on my screen
And I dream
dream
dream.

Sunlight beams its daytime reality of humidity and heat onto the Outback. I walk purposefully away from the chatter and bustle of the antenatal clinic towards the small room on the back verandah of the cattle station's homestead. I invert the small jar I'm carrying and the first urine sample of the day makes its shock entry into the life of outback plumbing. Pale yellow liquid splashes into the dirt-stained pan of the toilet and the water stirs. The head of a large goanna silently surfaces like a monster from the deep and blinks its shuttered eyes in the gloom of the bowl. 'Who goes there?' he seems to say, or maybe it's she. I keep pouring, blink back in surprise and mutter: 'Good morning to you too.' It's just as well I don't shock easily. I've seen larger goannas, but not in a toilet. The shuttered eyes close, the water ripples and he's gone again, round the bend.

This was my introduction to community health nursing and the first of many new experiences I had in the semi-arid, tropical Kimberley region of Western Australia. My entry into this new way of life would be full of questions, but I had hoped my first query might be more erudite than, *to flush or not to flush?* I made my way back to the clinic on the front verandah.

'All OK?' asked Marie.

'Yes, thanks,' I replied, picking up the next two samples for disposal. Later I say, 'There's a goanna in the toilet.'

'Yes, there often is.'

'I flushed it.'

'That's what I do.' We both smiled broadly and I seem to have made a friend.

My mentor Marie was a friendly, efficient flight nurse who was an 'old hand', having been in the job for about six months. She organised the clinic, working alongside a doctor from Derby Regional Hospital. Marie became a close friend, and years later I was appointed Godmother to her first son Michael.

This first week of my new role as a field nurse was meant to orientate me to the work and the place, but at this beginning point I was feeling somewhat disorientated. I'd arrived in Derby the night before, but had opted to come on the clinic rather than have the day in the office. We continued with our day of providing medical services to the people on three cattle stations, Mount House, Gibb River and Mount Elizabeth, before flying back to Derby via the coast to avoid the gathering thunderclouds.

Mount House Station was established in the early 1900s close to the Adcock River and was a sizeable pastoral lease of several thousand square kilometres. Mount Elizabeth was also pioneered about the same time and Gibb River cattle station was established a little later. Station life was hard for these pioneering families and station managers, and they were always hospitable and pleased to see us.

The Kimberley region of Western Australia is the size of England, and the small town of Derby is the same distance from Perth as Moscow is from London. In 1975 the Perth-to-Derby route could be a four or six-hour flight, depending on the number of stops. The alternative was a three to four-day drive depending on the condition of the road, which was not yet fully sealed. In the 1920s the Perth-to-Derby service was the world's longest passenger airline route, and my much later journey had certainly felt long considering we'd not left the State of WA. I'd arrived at night and had no idea in what direction we'd flown on that first clinic morning, except that it couldn't be very far west or we'd be in the ocean.

It was as well that I landed in Derby after dark because people were known to take the next flight out. As we descended, the night sky blurred the sight of mudflats scoured by centuries of tidal flow and desiccating seasons, projecting a barrenness that belied their ecological significance. Sweat trickled down my body as I walked across the tarmac to the small arrival and departure building. The air was dense with hanging humidity and a background chorus of amorous frogs was singing optimistic arias. I collected my luggage from the baggage trolley that was wheeled in by an MMA (MacRobertson Miller Airlines) employee in khaki shirt and shorts. Marie met me, and we drove the 10km into town in a Toyota Land

Cruiser. My room was in a four-bedroomed house that served as hospital nurses' accommodation. Marie asked if I would like to have a day in the office on the following day or come with her to Mt House. You know my answer.

My concise diary recorded that first day as beginning at 5.30am and finishing at 7.30pm. It became one of many long, tiring days that I found fascinating and fulfilling, which made bearable the persistent bush flies and 40°C heat. These clinic flights gave us panoramic, birds-eye views of the ancient, majestic landscape, and I found these as enthralling as my encounters with settlers, jackaroos (cowboys) and Aboriginal clients; note, not called patients. On that first day, we ate lunch at Gibb River Station which was owned and run by the Russ brothers and their wives. We'd brought meat and salad supplied by Derby Hospital and sometimes we would leave this fresh produce for the hosts and eat whatever they provided.

Wiry but aging, Frank Lacy was with us, returning home to Mount Elizabeth Station after a week in hospital. He was exhausted by the time we taxied to a stop on Mt Elizabeth's dirt airstrip. His family and station employees were delighted to have him home, and after we'd treated a couple of station hands who were waiting at the airstrip, we headed back to Derby. Jo Russ from Gibb River returned with us as her third child was due the following week. Her first child had arrived at home and her second on the flight to the hospital, so we hoped she'd make it to town for this third delivery, and she did. Frank's tiredness was an indicator of his poor health and the following Sunday they radioed that his condition had deteriorated and I flew out with the Royal Flying Doctor Service (RFDS) to Mt Elizabeth to bring him into hospital. This time his wife came with him. That was my first weekend on call as a temporary flight nurse as we were short staffed. The North's approaching wet season was usually a time of reduced staffing levels and my appointed role quickly included other functions, which pleased me.

Over time I learned the Kimberley could be a dream or a nightmare, depending on one's attitude, stamina and expectations. The work had its frustrations and rewards, and the lifestyle of the North was not for the faint-hearted. The wet season was hot and humid and I became accustomed to sweat trickling down my arms and legs. I constantly itched from mosquito and sandfly bites and I reverted to habits I'd learned in Africa, such as checking my shoes before putting them on and being alert to local creepy crawlies, snakes, spiders and bull ants. In spite of all these irritants, I knew I'd found my niche in nursing in this mix of clinical work with disease prevention, early intervention and health promotion. I returned to the Kimberley time and again over the next fifteen years.

Why did I instantly love the Kimberley? Maybe something of the landscape reminded me of Africa and this became evident in my response to driving past flat open shrubland dotted with red five-foot high anthills. I tensed in anticipation of having to face off a rhino before realising there would be none. I felt at home in the wide-open spaces, distant horizons and contrasting seasons, and seeing an eclectic mix of people within their unique ways of life. Some say that remote places attract missionaries, mercenaries and misfits, the three Ms. Perhaps I was a bit different too as the product of a faded empire who didn't quite fit anywhere. Whatever the reason, my mind has often wandered around happy and sad memories that began with that first memorable clinic at the renowned Mount House cattle station.

Part of my orientation to this new, yet strangely familiar world was a guided tour of Derby's significant sites. Derby was a small town situated at the base of King Sound, and its population pattern fluctuated depending on the seasons. During the wet season, people from the cattle stations and outlying communities moved into town and some government workers returned south. During the dry season the opposite happened. I discovered that this fluctuation was helpful to our work as community nurses and helped us to catch up with the more elusive clients when they migrated into town during the Wet.

The centre of Derby had one main road, Loch Street, which led to the wharf. Clarendon Street ran parallel and housed more shops. Our habit after a day's work was to walk down to the wharf and along the long jetty to catch the sea breeze and watch the stunning sunset over the King Sound. The wooden jetty was horseshoe-shaped, extending over muddy mangrove swamps to accommodate the massive 11m (36 foot) tides. It was a favourite recreation spot where fishing lines were thrown for silver cobbler, shark and north-west salmon, and nets were dropped to catch the large mud crabs. We'd lean over the jetty rails mesmerised by the fast flow of incoming or outgoing tides. These tides remain Australia's greatest and the Southern Hemisphere's second highest. Derby is undoubtedly not a seaside resort and to find a good beach we'd drive two hours to Broome, on the opposite side of the Dampier Peninsula.

During my first week in Derby, Marie drove me 7km out of town to a huge boab tree with a 14.7m girth, estimated to be about 1500 years old. Africa has myths about baobab trees and Australian myths about the boab tree are similar. One goes like this:

The tree was happy until it saw its reflection in a pool of water. He complained to the creator about being made so large and unsightly. God became angry with the tree's complaining and turned it upside-down so it couldn't see its reflection. Ever since, the baobab has been repentant and has done good deeds for people.

The so-called good deed done by the Derby tree happened in the early days of settlement. Its large hollow trunk gave overnight shelter to chained and manacled Aboriginal prisoners who were brought into town before being charged and incarcerated away from their home 'country'. The tree received the name of Prison Boab Tree. I was curious how it would have felt for those prisoners, and ventured inside the tree's cave-like trunk. I sensed enveloping despair and anger, and became so uncomfortable that I hopped out rather smartly. Once I heard the history, I understood this experience and became more respectful of such places. I have a boab nut that depicts the story, carved by a respected elder from Mojanjum Community. The Prison Tree has since been cordoned off and is marked as an Aboriginal sacred site; a wise move.

Hearing about Derby's past began to bring home to me just how little I knew of Australia's early history, and I determined to find out more. Over time, I discovered an ugly history of abuse and arrogant injustice, entangled with white settlement and juxtaposing some well-intended mission ventures and ill-conceived government policies. It's an old story of pioneers and colonisers along with the ubiquitous missionaries, mercenaries and misfits. The clash of cultures and ideals that accompany exploration and possession of land causes so much suffering. My race is responsible for much of it, and yet it too has evolved from ancient invasions and migrations. We're all a victim of our heritage, which doesn't make it just or right for Australia's First Nation people who were oppressed. How little humanity has changed over the ages. I didn't know it then, but the irony of this story is that in the 21ˢᵗ century a more substantial prison was built close by that first old prison boab tree.

One of the reasons this particular boab tree has lived so long is that it sits over an aquifer and water was brought to the surface at Mayall's Bore. The nearby 120-metre-long water trough was built about 1910 and a windmill drove the pump that kept it full. Over the years, that trough watered thousands of cattle from surrounding cattle properties, all waiting to be shipped out. The water from the bore had a rich mineral content and was reputed to have therapeutic properties. But in 1975 it produced a health hazard. The wet soil around the trough was contaminated with hookworms that burrow into bare feet and enter a person's bloodstream. There was a health warning notice near the trough. Hookworm caused severe anaemia and we regularly tested and treated people for it, especially children.

Fitting in

During those first few weeks I shared a house close to the hospital in Clarendon Street with three nurses. They were enjoying their first taste of life away from home and their boyfriends had all but moved in, making it overcrowded and often noisy. I wasn't happy about this and looked in vain for other accommodation. I was rescued by two departing community health nurses who introduced me to people who became good friends, Mike and Dasee Gugeri and their friend Jock Ponton, an ex-Kenya man in his early 50s.

According to my note of the day, we all had 'an excellent evening' on that first visit of many. Soon after, I jumped at the opportunity to pay a small rent to live in their 30-foot caravan that sat under an enormous open-ended machine shed on their property in Villiers Street. It was while living here, opposite the exposed marshland that I was inspired to write my opening poem. Mike and Dasee and their three young daughters lived in rooms that had been built onto the mezzanine floor of another huge shed. Downstairs was Mike's well-equipped workshop; he was a mechanic. We all shared a brick bathroom and toilet that stood between the two sheds. Mike was raised in Broome and educated in Perth, and Dasee was once a flight nurse, raised and trained in Queensland. Nurses and teachers have long since proved to be ideal wives for the men of rural and remote regions of Australia. Mike was the first person who was brave, or foolish, enough to drive truckloads of gasoline fuel up the rough Gibb River Road in the 1950s. In one of life's quirky coincidences, the small unit I had rented on arrival in Perth was on Gugeri Street, Claremont; land that was once owned by Mike's forebears.

Most evenings I joined Dasee and Mike with their young daughters and Jock who was very much a part of the family, to sit in the courtyard around their unique outdoor Kimberley stone table. The table's centrepiece was an arrangement of mosquito repellant, ashtrays, a fly swat, and an assortment of bottle tops and corks. A green glass fishing buoy and an old Broome pearl diver's helmet hung from the rafters of the corrugated iron roof. This shelter had become a friendly 'local' for station managers whenever they were in town. Jock would puff on his pipe and yarn with Mike about his trucking business and tell tales about his past experiences working with the Main Roads Department. Occasionally an itinerant pilot would drop in, and one insisted on calling me 'Blossom', much to Jock's amusement. I drank brandy and dry or shandy, we laughed a lot and I was able to avoid joining the more transient, mainly govern-ment-employed society of Derby's small community. I was happy to be accepted or at least tolerated by the local population.

Mike and Jock knew the countryside well and sometimes I'd go camp-ing with the family beside a small river in the bush, well off the Gibb River Road. It was their secret place, and as Gabby, their eight-year-old daughter stood on the rocks by the sparkling waters of the stream she declared in awe, 'God made this pretty good, didn't he?' And I agreed.

Work

This new way of life unfolded before me in that first week and over time I learned more about the Aboriginal and non-Aboriginal residents who made up the West Kimberley's multifaceted mix of cultures and socio-economic divide. I lived with a foothold in several aspects of the place and rarely won-dered where my own life was heading.

Derby Community Health Service was based in an old weatherboard building on the corner of Dellewarr and Loch streets. Its grounds were shaded by a well-grown mango tree loved by the local children who would scuttle up its branches to snatch its fruit in season. This building was Holman House, so named for the previous district medical officer, Lawson Holman, who had lived there from 1956 until 1970. The building was once a classic, grand Kimberley house with a ventilation skirt and verandah with louvres. Doctor Holman's initiatives led to the establishment of the health service that employed me. Tales of his varied and adventurous career brought enjoyment to many over the years and I heard some of these from both clients and friends. He was innovative, saved lives and improved the health of many more. He practised before the popularity of litigation made doctors more cautious about trying a risky, last resort procedure when a life was at stake. Older community nurses recalled with pride how they'd baby-sat his son D'Arcy, who went on to become a noted professor and epidemiologist.

I had hit the ground running in those first months because three or four community health nurses left as planned. Norma, the most senior nurse, was away on holiday and this left Marie and me holding the fort. We covered the work of four nurses as best we could and longed for some respite. We heard the only way to get a break was to have a nervous breakdown and we joked about sending a Telex to head office in Perth asking when we could book in for ours. Then we kept working. Public health was busy as the client population had swelled as the Wet set in. The heavy rain disrupted the road transport from Perth when the De Grey River flooded south of Broome, leaving stranded people and the north's grocery supply delayed for weeks.

Although my role was that of field nurse, I occasionally offered to give Marie a break by taking her weekend duty of being on-call for emergency flights. Flight nurses in the Kimberley were employed by the Community Health Nursing service, and the Royal Flying Doctor Service was funded from the State of Victoria as they have a smaller Outback. The RFDS radio station in Derby was a vital lifeline for the region as well as housing the radio service for the School of the Air. The hospital doctors provided the medical service for medical emergencies and helped the flight nurse with the on-air medical schedules on weekdays. I learnt to do this radio schedule the hard way when Marie was delayed returning from a camping trip one weekend. She and some hospital nurses had driven to Geikie Gorge near Fitzroy Crossing, and their vehicle battery went flat overnight. This meant they couldn't radio for help, but as they had let someone know where they were going, they were rescued later on Monday. This was another lesson to be learned about life in the north – take plenty of water and let someone know where you're going and when you expect to return. And always stay with your vehicle. As I took on the radio schedule I was grateful for my late father's occupation that had familiarised me with radio etiquette and the alphabet.

Those first few weeks were full of clinic trips and emergency flights. We returned people discharged from the hospital and we brought back sick clients. To this day I remember the first client I returned to Fitzroy Crossing, his name was Hitler (no moustache). People had a range of illnesses and conditions: respiratory infections, renal pain, hypertension and antenatal women in their last four weeks of pregnancy. We administered treatment for Hansen's disease (leprosy), sexually transmissible diseases, intestinal infections and infestations (worms, giardia, gastroenteritis). We kept a lookout for listed leprosy patients who had scattered during the devastation of Darwin by Cyclone Tracy during Christmas 1974.

The unwelcome disease of syphilis became notable in the Kimberley around the time I arrived in 1975, although it was probably present long before. In 1986 some wag pointed out that HIV infections also reached Derby when I returned that year. Of course, neither was due to me but the coincidence amused a few. I was told the endemic presence of yaws had probably afforded protection against syphilis and once yaws was controlled by antibiotics people became more vulnerable to syphilis. HIV infections may have arrived earlier than 1986, but I was the person in Derby who was first approached by someone concerned to be tested. No one knew the protocols and the hospital laboratory technician made multiple phone calls to Perth for advice. The outcome of this was for me to be sent to Perth's Sexual Health Clinic to learn more about HIV protocols and procedures. My eyes were opened to much more besides. The person who had inadvertently exposed our ignorance of the correct procedures was clear of HIV.

⌐⁓

Marie and I played a lot of Scrabble. Television was yet to make its entry into the homes of the North and the Australian Broadcasting Corporation (ABC) radio programme assumed all its listeners were sports enthusiasts. It broadcast Aussie Rules Football in the southern winter and cricket in summer, and I struggled with the rules of both. The Derby Outdoor Picture

Theatre brought relief from Scrabble and the ABC. Its outdoor venue was shielded by a high fibro fence that was broken in places with child-size gaps. Inside it was filled with rows of sagging deckchairs that we would lower ourselves into with caution, in case they split. The system was to pay on entry, sit wherever you liked and bring your refreshments. We sat in front of the large screen, well behind the excited, bickering small children who sat right at the front of the chairs on the ground. We had armed ourselves with Aerogard (tropical strength), sandfly deterrent, a cushion or two and an 'esky' (cooler) of drinks and nibbles. Everyone munched and drank through the film.

The town's favourite films were Westerns when the Aboriginal audience was eager to cheer the Indians and boo the cowboys. The best experience for me was when *The Sting* was shown. Most of the community loved playing cards and gambling, which meant the bulk of the audience understood every nuance of Robert Redford's scam and every move of the poker game. They cheered and 'ooh-ed and aah-ed in delight. I'm not a poker player, so the audience response helped me to make some sense of it all. Chatter about the film's sequences went on in the local communities for weeks. If only Paul Newman's beautiful blue eyes could have seen us, I think he would have enjoyed the audience participation.

In that first year, many 'mercy flights' were declared by the hospital doctors. This was an authorised evacuation of someone with a life-threatening condition when Civil Aviation's advice was not to fly because of the bad weather and the plane's lack of instruments. The on-duty doctor would authorise a mercy flight and then deem it unnecessary for a doctor to go. The pilot and nurse were sent out in dangerous weather and flying conditions. I became angry about this, declaring:

'If it's bad enough to declare a mercy flight then it's bad enough to need a doctor.'

I was especially disgruntled after a mercy flight in which pilot Jan Ende started talking wistfully about his wife and young children. Lighting flashed to left and right of us as Jan flung the RFDS Beechcraft Baron around the worst of the thunderclouds.

'You watch out that side and I'll watch this one,' he shouted above the noise.

Watch for lightning, I assumed. It was a terrifying flight. Sadly, the child with meningitis who we brought back from Balgo Hills died in hospital the following week. We all could have died, as had happened to one nurse and crew years before. When I returned to the Kimberley in 1979, I discovered that the rule had changed and all mercy flights had to have a doctor on board. Maybe my voice had been joined by others. Fewer mercy flights were declared.

There were two Aboriginal communities whose health clinics became my responsibility during the year. One was Mowanjum and the other Looma. **Mowanjum** community was established near Derby in 1956 when the Presbyterian church moved the residents of Wotjulum Mission to a new site near Derby. Until 1963, children at Mowanjum were under the guardianship of the Commissioner of Native Welfare, and by 1971, 65 school-age children were living within the community. Mowanjum became a self-governing community in 1972, and I became their community nurse in 1975. When I returned to Derby in 1979, they had moved to a new site off the Gibb River Road near Derby, in part because the old site was infested by hookworm. In later years their art centre developed and thrived, producing beautiful artworks that sell overseas and locally.

The community's proximity to town didn't help the problem that arose with alcohol abuse. On my return in 1980, I met up with an intellectually disabled girl I'd known five years before. I recently found a disquieting poem I wrote as I grieved for her disintegrated life:

Oh Ida, I see you.
What chance did you have?
Not the full quid.

Abused as a kid
Oh Ida, I see you.
*

A woman, black,
flat on your back
for the price of a drink.
It pays not to think?
Oh, Ida I see you.

How did she come to this? The pain of it tore at me and the sense that I and others had failed her, sat heavily on my heart.

Looma Community was the second community I regularly visited in 1975. Their gathering place was about 115km south of Derby, off the Fitzroy Crossing Road near Camballin.

'Why have they chosen this place to build their community?' I asked our well-respected senior nurse, Norma, who had returned from holiday by then.

'Look for the three hills behind the rear boundary. There's a Dreamtime story about the hills that relates to the people. It's about a blue tongue lizard and her children. Ask about it when you get to know some of the older women.'

'So, they're all from the same language group?'

'They're all interrelated and have cultural bonds, but some of the languages may be different. I'm not sure because some were still working on Liveringa Station and some were in the (Aboriginal) reserves.'

I began to understand why there was an increase in the movement of people away from their usual homelands that they referred to as 'my Country'. It was only five years since equal wages had been introduced in 1968-69. The pastoralists were unused to paying all their workforce and the economic impact on them led to the eviction of Aboriginal families and older workers from the stations, forcing them to leave their traditional country. The people had no choice but to congregate in makeshift camps close to small towns – Fitzroy Crossing, Halls Creek, Derby and Broome. The effects could be seen in the poverty, squalor and the burden of disease in these places. The development of independent communities was part of the solution and was funded by the Federal Labor government of the day.

Looma's community of large, interrelated families began in 1970 as a result of these evictions. When we arrived to set up the clinic, the families were being housed under bright blue tents while the community's houses were being built by employed local men under the supervision of skilled builders. Nancy, the health worker, and I had left Derby about 6am to beat the heat of the day and were set up in the shade of a lone large tree by 8am. The folding table and two chairs were placed close to the rear doors of our 4x4 vehicle that we'd loaded and fuelled up the evening before. First, we walked around the camp greeting people and checking that clients on our long treatment list were there. The wet season was a time for gatherings and ceremonies, and we noticed a 'few mobs' of people from other areas had remained after a big corroboree the previous week. By 11am the people's morning was done and they disappeared to their tents or the river. We had to work quickly to do everything that needed to be done; immunisations for the children, Hansen's disease checks for others and various treatments for common conditions and minor injuries. During lunch it was usual for us to go down to Liveringa river crossing. Nancy was often with me, and she always jumped into the river to cool off.

'Come on, Sister.' I jumped in fully clothed.

'What about crocodiles?' I asked during my first trip, as I splashed around enjoying the cool.

'They're only little ones.' She laughed as I leapt out. In my book there were no harmless crocodiles, but I did note that the freshwater Johnstone crocodiles were much smaller than the monsters around the coast and those in the African rivers and lakes.

I learnt so much from Nancy, who was a pretty, intelligent young woman from Broome. She interpreted the culture and guided my under-standing of cultural norms, body language and a few useful words. It was Nancy who explained to me, when I couldn't find a male client, that I'd been put into a 'skin', or kinship group, that prohibited him from looking at me. Or me him, apparently. It was Nancy who smoothed the way for me so that I gained acceptance by other health workers and sections of the general community. She also told me about some bush medicines.

'This leaf is good for scabies; girls use that one to stop babies.'

She would occasionally 'go walkabout' for a few days and I gleaned from our conversations that the reason for her absence was often boyfriends and parties as well as cultural obligations. She eventually completed her training as an enrolled nurse, which was a big achievement for anyone who likes to 'go walkabout'. I understood the need for downtime, but our different priorities and work ethic was a source of frustration, as it usually is for most non-indigenous people. I admired all the health workers for their grace and patience with us and the steady stream of culturally ignorant medical and nursing personnel who came and went.

The final episode for this chapter springs to life after a more recent Kimberley holiday at Cape Leveque, which today offers an upmarket camp resort near the tip of the Dampier Peninsula. It proclaims itself to be a place of *astonishing diversity, pristine wilderness and unique landscape,* and offers *a once in a lifetime experience.*

It was all that it claimed, but for me it was a 'thrice in a lifetime' experience. The first time was on a Saturday in 1975 when humidity was at 99 per cent and temperatures above 40°C. I was at home recovering from Friday's clinic trip, which had been my first solo clinic run with the RFDS and had included a long aircraft diversion for an emergency evacuation. We had departed from Derby on time, flown to Broome where we left Dr Ken and health worker Dotty to do the school medicals and picked up the Broome doctor and community health nurse. We then flew to Lombadina and Beagle Bay missions on the Dampier Peninsula. While at Lombadina the plane, pilot and I were diverted to an emergency evacuation from Louisa Downs, about 76km east of Derby. We refuelled at Derby and collected a fresh flask of tea from the thoughtful Marie and flew on to retrieve the sick child. Having delivered him to a waiting ambulance at Derby airport, we returned to Beagle Bay to collect the doctor and nurse and returned them to Broome in exchange for Ken and Dotty. They added plants, fish and fresh bread to the plane's load. Friday had become a 1000km round trip and no wonder I was relaxing at home on Saturday. But I was also on-call and had a feeling I would be called. I'm not the only nurse who experienced this type of foreknowledge. The phone call came from pilot Jan Ende at 6pm, after he had been alerted via Perth on an international frequency.

'There's a very sick child at Cape Leveque. No time to change, get yourself to the airport NOW.' I notified the hospital and had the RFDS hanger doors open by the time Jan arrived at the airport. He was impressed, and from then he trusted me to do a good job. At Cape Leveque airstrip we were met by Sister Anne (McGlynn) and Brother Bob who'd travelled by road from Lombadina. The child was the daughter of the lighthouse keeper and his wife. We did a quick turnaround and had her with her mother in Derby Hospital by 8pm. The little girl was in theatre by 10pm that night, having almost ruptured her appendix. I must confess that it was quite a buzz, but I was never a natural emergency nurse and was proud to have coped so well. Training will out.

My holiday to Cape Leveque in 2017 was not an emergency, although I did take a nasty tumble through a broken wooden step while visiting Lombadina and could have needed a flight out. But all was well and I was spared the experience of being a patient rather than the nurse. There was no need for a lighthouse keeper when automatic lights were installed in the 1980s. In another of those quirky coincidences of life, my more recent friend Judy spent some of her childhood at Cape Leveque when her parents were lighthouse keepers there in the 1960s. All Australia's lighthouses were automated by the mid-1990s.

⌒

Throughout all these adventures in the Kimberley, another beginning was rumbling away inside me. It related to my early Christian faith and was

helped along by several encounters and circumstances. My nursing colleague Marie was a committed Christian and I met several Christian pilots
on the occasions I relieved Marie over the weekends. Whenever the RFDS
pilot was out of hours, meaning he'd exceeded his weekly quota of flying
hours, the emergency flights were provided by a Derby-based air charter
company, Aerial Enterprises. The owner Dick Roberton was a man of faith
and employed young Christian pilots who were gaining experience and flying hours before serving overseas with Mission Aviation Fellowship. It was
one of these pilots who managed to catch me in a weak moment and get me
to church.

We had returned to Derby airport after an emergency flight to One Arm
Point to bring back a sick child. I made my way to the waiting ambulance
carrying the child in my arms, my flight bag over my shoulder and the
portable oxygen cylinder in the free hand. The pilot, Neil, approached and
reached for the cylinder.

'I'll carry the oxygen if you come to church with me on Sunday. Come
on, give it here, Audrey.'

I handed over the cylinder without thinking. 'All right.'

It wasn't until I'd taken the child to outpatients, seen her settled, finished unpacking at the office and was on my way home that I realised what
I'd done. *Idiot. Look what you've let yourself in for now. Well, I'm not going to
let any Christian think an agnostic can't keep her word.*

So, there I was on Sunday sitting with Neil at the evening service in
Derby's Aboriginal People's Church singing choruses, fumbling with pages
of the Bible and feeling like a foreigner in a vaguely familiar land. Nairobi
Cathedral and St Ebbes in Oxford had not been quite like this.

This began a six-month journey to such a deep inner renewal and commitment to Jesus that I've never turned away from him since. During that
process I reviewed my personal life, realised the mess I was making of it
and decided to let God have a go. Maybe he or she could help me make
better sense of it. This decision marked the closure of my first year in the
Kimberley. I refused an opportunity to receive a government scholarship
for a new advanced nursing course in Perth, and instead I applied to attend

a theological college in New Zealand. The quirky coincidences of life are often God-given opportunities for a rethink.

Reflection

The joy of finding God has outweighed the pleasure of finding a place I loved. We often hesitate to leap into what we see as the unknown, of place and religion. Both these adventures proved to be life-changing and fulfilling. 'He who hesitates is lost,' or as the Bible says: This is what I shall tell my heart, and so recover hope: the favours of Yahweh are not all passed, his kindnesses are not exhausted. They are new every morning. Lamentations 3:21-22

Ten

ADVENTURES IN FAITH

Lord, make me an instrument of your peace;
where there is hatred, let me sow love;
where there is injury, pardon;
where there is discord, union;
where there is doubt, faith;
where there is despair, hope;
where there is darkness, light;
and where there is sadness, joy.
A Prayer of St. Francis of Assisi extracted from https://en.wikisource.org/wiki/ on
10/8/2018.

'I may be wrong, but I know I'm right.' This mantra of Christian certitude offered by the Derby People's Church preacher rankled me each time he threw it into the congregation. After first being bribed to come to church, I began to attend voluntarily with my pilot friend Neil. Words of faith bounced around the room, in hope of finding a receptive ear, but only the ageing overhead fan creaked a response. Neil looked sideways at me as I contained a sigh.

I don't see how he can be so sure. I took out my frustration on a hovering mosquito, slap! *Got you.*

Along the aisle, the youngest Roberton child captured a cicada, and smiling mischievously, unfurled its wings and stretched them out. The creature's shrill response to this indignity shattered the urgency of the preacher's final words, and the final rousing hymn drowned out the poor cicada's grief. His older sister rescued the creature as his mother approached me.

'Audrey, would you like to come to lunch?' she asked.

'I'd love to, thank you.'

These lunches became a significant part of my return to faith as they offered hospitality, kindness and helpful conversations. I was on edge waiting for someone to tell me I was a sinner, something I would have hotly denied. But no one did and all I received was friendship and a welcome into the family's home. Meals at the Robertons were mostly outdoor events at a long wooden table, and we were joined by visiting bishops, politicians, pilots and waifs and strays like me. Many new friendships were established over the washing up, and for this reason it was years before a dishwasher was installed. Later into our friendship, I borrowed a Bible from Joan, and in the privacy of my rented caravan opposite the marsh, I began my research. It was time for me to decide whether I'd continue making the poor decisions that messed up my life or let God take over. I'd heard the gospel message often enough to know I had a choice to make. Even so, I wanted some clear indication of the truth that Jesus was the Son of God and necessary to my life. I began in the Old Testament book of the prophet Isaiah, reasoning that if an old prophecy were shown to come true in the New Testament, then it would be an excellent first step. I began to read in secret at home because I wasn't ready to be questioned and may have been ridiculed. I sat at my dining table reading and in case someone called in unexpectedly, I hid the Bible behind the covers of a less-than-wholesome women's magazine *Cosmopolitan*.

An epiphany happened as I read the first eight verses of chapter six where Isaiah described his vision of being confronted by the holiness of God.

[5] *'Woe to me!' I cried, 'I am ruined! For I am a man of unclean lips, and I live among a people of unclean lips, and my eyes have seen the King, the Lord Almighty.'* [6] *Then one of the seraphim flew to me with a live coal in his hand, which he had taken with tongs from the altar.* [7] *With it, he touched my mouth*

and said, 'See, this has touched your lips; your guilt is taken away, and your sin atoned for.'

These words stirred something at the core of my inner being and a small flame flickered at the embers of my faith. I felt deeply disturbed and understood this to be a time when I needed to decide one way or the other. Sitting at my dining table, I prayed for help to understand and believe. Over the following days I shifted my reading to the New Testament gospel accounts of Jesus's life and waited to see what might happen. I felt surprisingly peaceful about it all.

What people may not know is that during the mid-1970s there was a revival, a move of the Holy Spirit sweeping through churches of several denominations across many countries including Australia and New Zealand. It was known as the Charismatic Movement. The Spirit renewed people's faith in Christ, brought new converts and had an enduring effect on the life of the Church. It was viewed with suspicion by some Christians and embraced by others, causing tensions in some churches that ended with their congregations splitting into two separate churches. But overall, this movement re-energised lukewarm and nominal Christians. Since those years, I've met active Christians in small rural churches who tell me they found faith or affirmed their flagging faith during the 1970s. It's not surprising that I was caught up in this godly breeze and holy fire, especially as my own converted family had persisted in praying for me.

Friends and colleagues in Derby became part of this holy bombardment. These included the St John of God nursing nuns, my nurse friend Marie and my Pentecostal boss. One weekend I travelled with them to Broome and a small gathering of Roman Catholic and Pentecostal Christians, an unusual combination.

'Would you like us to pray for you to be filled with the Spirit, Audrey?' the nuns asked.

'If there's more, then yes please,' I responded with some trepidation, recalling that fools rush in where angels fear to tread.

I sat upright on my chair and three or four women laid hands on me while they prayed for me. Nothing dramatic happened and they seemed disappointed, persisting until I relaxed into a warm sense of peace. We sang for the whole two-hour trip back to Derby that day.

I realised much later that this was a significant turning point in my journey and in my identity. Where I came from became less important as I grew in the assurance of being beloved by God. I became thirsty for scriptural knowledge and my search changed from one of 'is it true?' to 'I need to know and understand more.'

Like any thinking person, I've reflected on the mystery of faith and these early months of Christian growth. I've been through times of doubt, but have found that those times served to lead me to more understanding, not less faith. This has been my journey and we're all unique in the way we make sense of life and travel our inner journeys.

In the flush of my renewed faith I was determined to speak out to all those for whom I cared. I let family and friends know I was now a committed Christian and waited for their responses. Some friends had also been rethinking their childhood beliefs, and we encouraged one another. Others asked questions and tried to understand, but most viewed my dive into the deep end of belief as a lunatic leap overboard. My friend and love from Kenya said it was 'inevitable', but didn't explain his comment. By then he was a psychiatrist, and I may not have understood his explanation. His father had been a lay preacher in the Highlands of Scotland, and I'd hoped he might understand without the psychoanalysis. Maybe his father's zeal had rendered him immune. My Derby friend Jock, an older Scot, went a step further and gave me a copy of the Koran with a note written on its flyleaf, 'to seek, to strive, to find and not to yield'. All comments were well intended, and I knew they came out of friendship. None dissuaded me.

It was when I gave up alcohol that some friends became really rattled. Word went out, and a few took to sending a fore-runner to warn the hostess, 'Audrey doesn't drink anymore'. Not that I was much of a drinker in the first place, so this puzzled me. It was 20 years before I had another drink and by then I was no longer working with people whose families and communities were being destroyed by alcohol abuse. When I eventually broke my God-imposed abstinence, it seemed appropriate that I was out to dinner with an Anglican priest.

Bible College

Theological studies were the natural progression in my search for more understanding. I wasn't identifying with a specific Protestant denomination and chose an interdenominational college. The Bible College of New Zealand, now called Laidlaw College in Auckland, offered me a place at short notice. There was an unexpected vacancy, just as there had been when I chose general nursing and then midwifery training. I once again encountered more learning, the least of which was the New Zealand accent.

'Have you got a pin, Audrey?'

'Sorry, no.'

'Yes, you have, there's one in your pocket.'

'Oh, this? A PEN!'

'That's what I said; a pin.'

It took a while for me to decipher the nuances of yet another version of the English language. My college friends teased Australian students for their accent and mine confused them. I was asked to repeatedly to say the word *holy* which seemed to amuse them. My vowels had obviously become an unusual mixture of past speaking influences. Alongside Australians, the students were New Zealanders, including Maori, as well as Samoan, South Korean, Iranian and Singaporean – people of diverse social and professional backgrounds unified by one faith. My time at the college was a joy and a struggle. I had much to learn about myself, biblical truths and theological conundrums, and this was the beginning of lifelong learning. We were part of the college work team and helped in the orchard, kitchen, dining room and general cleaning as delegated by a roster. In my second year, I opted to take on the flower arranging and had a great time making large arrangements for the main hall and smaller ones around the college to soften the environment.

'Happy Birthday, Audrey!' Two girls knocked on my door as the 'pups' (pips) signalled breakfast, my least favourite meal. This noisy early morning ritual in the main dining room jarred and became my daily challenge to gracious acceptance. My friends walked with me to the small lounge at the end of the girls' accommodation wing. Breakfast was being served away from the hubbub of the main dining room. A small gathering of women put love into action by giving me the gift of gentle start to the day.

A month later, I was called to the front office: 'Audrey, you have visitors.'

'Really? How strange,' and I hurried across the central courtyard.

'Surprise!' called out two distant figures. It was Zena and Bill, my Mombasa friends who'd retired home to New Zealand. It certainly was a surprise. It became apparent as we chatted and I showed them around that they'd come with some notion that I needed to be rescued from some dreadful mistake. It was well meant but distressing for me.

'Everyone looks so miserable,' bemoaned Zena.

'Really? They're just going to their next lecture.' And somehow in that time, we lost our connection. Our lives were on divergent paths.

College learning was also practical, and once a week I would join a group that helped at a drop-in café in the centre of Auckland. From there I would accompany a more mature Christian man to visit a 'doss house', or cheap hostel for homeless people, many of whom were caught up in cycles of drug or alcohol abuse. It was not pleasant with its long dimly lit corridor of small rooms. The middle-aged man we usually visited was unkempt, odorous and often hungover. He was a sorry sight lying sprawled under worn dirty sheets, but he was always pleased to see us. No matter what was done to help him he'd return to this same state and his hopelessness stuck in my mind. I'd seen the seedier side of life through my nursing years so was not shocked, but always saddened.

These visits and the café were invaluable experiences both practically and spiritually. I sat with people whose lives had become so mired in dross that they believed themselves unworthy of anyone's attention, let alone God's. I experienced the power of God over evil as Satan worshippers tried to invade the café's space. College was more than book learning, and grounded me in these unexpected ways. I learned the basics of teaching and put them into practice on a class of ten-year-old boys at a local primary school. My mentor was a ventriloquist and could control the class with the promise of bringing his doll and performing for them at the end of the term. I had no such gift to offer, and survived the following year without a mentor by always keeping the troublemakers involved, active and busy.

Throughout the college semesters, I attended a Maori church that had services akin to the People's Church in Derby. The people themselves were different from the Australian Aboriginal but had the same culture of family and sharing. I enjoyed the Maori people for their generous and open hearts, and their musical ability. The teenagers enlightened me that I often sang flat, and the cheerful pastor's occasional joke was to pronounce Audrey as Ordinary. Ha! Ha!

The college's mid-year break was usually a time to help with external ministries like the Australian Scripture Union children's camps. I was on a team that went to the South Island outside Christchurch in the most beautiful countryside and we were treated to a jetboat ride on a fast-flowing local river. The week involved small group sessions and worship services each morning before the day's activities began. I was the camp nurse. In my second year of college I joined a team north of Auckland in a small beachside community that was predominately Maori. During one of these camps, a mini-revival broke out among the young boys. They repeatedly came to the team leaders saying they wanted to ask Jesus into their hearts. The leaders needed great wisdom in handling this event and each child was counselled to consider their decision a little longer. Most returned the next day still wanting to declare their faith. At the end of the camp, the leaders visited the parents of these children to discuss any concerns they had and to seek their permission for their child to go to a nearby Sunday school. Some parents didn't want a bar of it and refused outright, others agreed, and several parents followed their children and became regular churchgoers.

Return to the Kimberley

During the college's Christmas break I returned to Derby and was employed at Numbala Nunga Nursing Home. I knew the matron, who appreciated that I needed to earn enough for my next year's college fees and gave me the shifts that attracted the higher 'penalty rates'. I worked many evening and night shifts, including public holidays. Numbala Nunga had previously been a small Presbyterian Church-owned hospital. In 1977 it was managed by the Health Department of Western Australia and held about 30 patients, providing residential and respite care to traditional Aboriginal men and women. Some elderly, unwell 'white fella' cattle station workers with no known relatives were also given care. Their lives had been rough and one of them used to go to great lengths to avoid having a shower. The Kimberley Aboriginal men spoke their languages and bore chest markings indicating status and old cultural law ceremonies. A few had 'whistle-cock' penises, an opening in the underside of the shaft. It was difficult to know how much of their behaviour was normal, dementia or distress at being out of their usual environment.

My time at Numbala Nunga during the college holidays taught me not to judge but respect vulnerable displaced people in spite of their stomach-wrenching habits. After my first experience of the dining room meal time, I prayed I would be able to empathise and care for my patients. I grew to enjoy them, but meal times continued to challenge me as I helped to feed the more disabled and deal with the noise, incontinence and the women's habit of storing little wads of food behind their ears for later. The nursing aides dealt with all this without batting an eye, and I was almost at that point by the time I went back to college.

Away from their people, land and normal bush camp environment these older adults were coping as best as they knew how within this place and stage of life. Their life histories went back at least 80 years, and I wished I knew their language and could hear their stories. The nursing home was adjusting as fast as it could to provide more cultural comfort. It can't have been that bad an experience because I returned to work there after my time at college and in Sydney.

Towards the end of my second year at college, students were to decide which direction their lives would take. There was no obvious pressure, but there was an unspoken expectation that we'd serve in a Christian mission or church. I'd gone to Bible college to remedy my lack of grounding in Christianity, but I was open to full-time Christian work as long as it wasn't nursing overseas. I was also reticent about joining a 'faith mission' that expected the missionary to raise their financial support. My sister Frances and her husband Max were working with Africa Inland Mission among the Maasai people in Kenya and I disagreed with their mission's approach of seeking financial support. Frances and Max spent most of their holidays asking congregations for pledges of money. They needed to raise the equivalent of the British basic wage. I prefer the Church Missionary Society approach where the organisation raises funds, pays and supports their missionaries, freeing them of the worry and allowing them to get on with their work.

I'd done well in my college exams, except for my last semester of Greek. I'd found a riveting biography to read on the night before exams, and my revision suffered. This love of books led me to consider work with a literature mission, Christian Literature Crusade (CLC). I thought I might attach a little more adventure to my choice by seeing if I could go to Liberia in West Africa. This plan providentially fell through and about a year later Liberia fell into civil strife and became an unsafe country. Instead, I returned to England to visit family before arriving at CLC headquarters in West Pennant Hills, Sydney in February 1978.

Sydney

I was one of seven candidates in training and we lived on campus for an initial six months. Working in a warehouse full of Christian books was my greatest delight, and we were expected to read them, which was even better. I devoured the many genres, from novels to study books, self help books on Christian living and biographies. We attended tutorials and assisted in the bookshop. Eventually, the board met to decide if we were suitable to join the mission. I'd hoped to take on a mobile bookshop and was disappointed when this was turned down; I couldn't do this alone. Instead, I remained living on campus and took on management of one of the Sydney CLC shops, which was in Chatswood. I was pleased with the experience but felt like a caged lion in the city, and driving in heavy traffic one morning I decided it was time to return to nursing and the Kimberley. Little did I realise that this move would lead me into yet another adventure and country.

The way in which I made decisions had changed by this time – I prayed about them. My motivation had shifted towards Christian service, but not necessarily as a part of a missionary society.

Reflection

Describing an intimate relationship in the physical world is never easy. Explaining a spiritual connection with Jesus is even more difficult. The mind is as engaged as the heart, and there's a spiritual shift in some inner core of one's being. Some people have believed from childhood and grow in faith; others have dramatic conversions. Mine seems to have been a mixture of both. Life with God at the helm is a wonderful adventure.

Eleven

DE FACTO MISSIONARY

Three things I said I'd never be;
a nurse, a teacher, a missionary.
And here I am, doing all three.
'Ha! Ha!' says God, the Trinity.

The first two Anglican missionaries to the people of Papua New Guinea's Milne Bay region arrived by boat from England via Australia in 1890. I came by small aircraft a century later in 1980. Copeland King and Albert Maclaren were sent by the Church and I was sent by the charity Save the Children Fund, but God had a hand in both our arrivals. My flight from Alotau, the main regional town, was on a Beechcraft Islander aircraft that took fifteen minutes to transport me over the mountainous and densely vegetated terrain of the Owen Stanley Ranges to Dogura. The coastal route would have taken me three days, but that would still have been a shorter voyage than that of King and Maclaren. We probably all arrived with some trepidation.

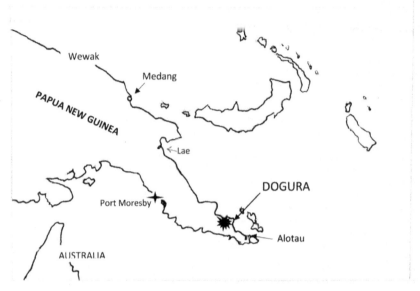

Papua New Guinea, showing Dogura

The mission station of Dogura was founded by King, a year after his colleague Maclaren died. I mention Maclaren because the Mission's launch carried his name. King landed on the beach at Wamira, near Wedau village and he was permitted to build a house on the Dogura plateau behind Wedau. This was a barren acreage used only for tribal fighting.

As the plane's wing dipped in descent, I peered down at the place where I was to work and live for three years. Scattered around what appeared to be a large village green, were a mix of buildings dwarfed by an incongruous edifice that I recognised from photographs. This was the concrete masonry of the European-style Cathedral of Saints Peter and Paul, and the size of it in this remote location astonished me. It shone stark white in the morning sunshine and was the largest Anglican church in the country, holding 800 people (although not 800 seats). It was consecrated in 1939, three years before the outbreak of war in the South Pacific and went on to survive the traumatic Japanese occupation of Papua New Guinea in World War II. The cathedral has a plaque within it from the Japanese, presented as an apology and token of reconciliation.

A shiver of excitement raced through me as I stepped down from the plane onto the grassy runway. The mountains behind now looked deceptively benign, and turning around my eyes were drawn to the ocean vista of deep blue, and I smiled with pleasure. I was greeted by Rolf, the mission's administrator, and Lesley, the principal of St Barnabas School of Nursing, my new boss. The mission's open truck ferried us up the hill to my accommodation. The house was surrounded by fruiting mango trees and held four bedrooms, a lounge, outside toilet and a bathroom with a bucket shower. The kitchen was in a separate building nearby. I shared this house with Rolf, a bachelor from South Australia, and Jessie, a Sri Lankan widow who taught domestic science at the Holy Name High School on the other side of the mission campus. Another West Australian in his early 60s arrived with me and left within the week. It was not what he'd expected. Nothing I'd seen so far fazed me and I entered this new adventure with eager anticipation, despite my usual nervousness in a new job.

This move had opened for me after my time in Sydney with CLC and while I was again working in the Kimberley. A colleague had pointed out an advertisement in her current Save the Children Fund magazine. It was for a post in Uganda and suddenly I was restless again. My sister Frances was horrified that I should consider going to Uganda, with its current political instability and violence. Her concern and the potential danger caused me to examine the extent of my trust in God. Was I willing to take the risk or was this one adventure too far? The inner pull to apply increased and I sent off my letter, leaving the outcome to Save the Children Fund and God. I was informed the position had been filled by the UK branch of the agency and I thought, *that was a strange exercise in faith.*

I continued my life in the Kimberley until a month later I received a phone call from Perth asking me to consider going to Papua New Guinea. This country was familiar to many Australians, but not a place I'd felt any particular pull towards. Yet here was a call to contribute once again to an underdeveloped nation. The position was that of sister tutor and despite my lack of formal qualifications as a nurse educator, I was offered it and accepted. I knew something of adult learning and the principles of teaching through promoting health and my Bible college training. It was January 1980 when I began taking anti-malarials, packed my bag with nursing text books, water purifying tablets and a few clothes and flew to Port Moresby via Brisbane. After a day in Port Moresby at the rectory of a friendly Anglican priest I flew to Alotau on the national airline Talair.

Alotau airport's arrivals and departure lounge was a hut on the edge of the airstrip that proclaimed itself to be the Gurney International Airport, Milne Bay. It was built during World War II by a United States engineers regiment. Strangely, it was in this hut two years later that I bumped into a boyfriend from my Kenya days. Lofty was short in stature and long in sur-name and fidelity. He'd migrated to Australia and had contacted me some years earlier to ask me to join him in New Ireland, an island in Papua New Guinea where he was working. Now here he was, working for the Electoral Commission and waiting for his flight to Port Moresby. A weird coincidence or a God moment? I remained ambivalent about this friendship, although Lofty's affection remained.

After my first landing at Gurney, I travelled to Alotau on the airport bus and was delighted to find myself once again in a tropical setting with a sandy, palm-lined road that reminded me of Mombasa. St Barnabas School of Nursing had a training base in Alotau's government hospital that included two Canadian doctors and a small operating theatre. The main sec-tion of the Anglican nurse training school was in Dogura, where there was a smaller mission hospital with fewer facilities and no permanent doctor. I spent some days in Alotau with Sally, an English midwife and mission-ary, before I winged my way to Dogura. In that time, I learned a few more nursing skills that had not been part of my Western training, like incising abscesses. I also mastered carrying my billum, a locally made string bag, by placing its strap across my forehead and dropping the bag onto my back. This method was similar to what I knew from Africa. I would walk up hills with my shopping, leaning forward to make the load easier. It still took me longer than most people to get up the hills and I hoped this would improve with practice; it didn't.

As I recalled these days, a plethora of memories of Dogura nudged me and clamoured for supremacy. The sounds and smells of yet another tropical location mingled with the tolling of the Angelus bell from the cathedral tower that stopped work across the campus; a call to prayer or at least reflection at 6am, midday and 6pm. These reminded me of the mosque calls in Mombasa that I'd heard eight years before. Then there were the night sounds of village pigs foraging among the fallen mangos and the sweet smell of the ripe fruit. I enjoyed it all and even grew used to sitting on the cold cement slabs of the cathedral floor for services. During long sermons in the local language, I amused myself watching the bishop's dog boss the village dogs into submission. I was spiritually sustained by the words and tunes of the old hymns. However, I was less inspired by their Easter traditions and the Good Friday three-hour trek around the Stations of the Cross that meant listening to a full-length sermon at each station, in various languages, in the heat of the day.

Being on call at night was also a less enjoyable memory. There'd be the sound of footsteps padding down the path from the hospital at two in the morning. I'd be alert in a flash and at the front door before the student nurse arrived with his request.

'Sister Audrey, please can you come?'

'What is it Simon?'

'Sister Margaret wants you to come.'

This usually meant a woman's labour was going wrong. I'd arrive at the labour ward where the sound of the manually operated suction pump would tell me that a baby has been born or was about to be. I'd check the baby was breathing and then palpate the woman's abdomen.

'I think there's another one to come,' I might say.

'Yes, sister. We thought there was.' And all went well as the second twin was born.

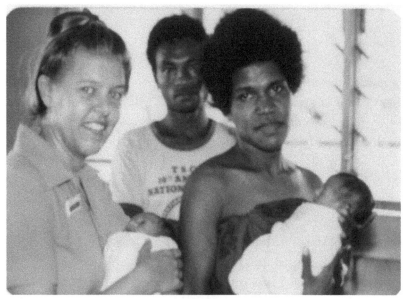

A safe delivery

The path between the house and hospital must be the most prayed-up area of the mission grounds. Once again, the nurses hadn't given me their clinical findings until I'd confirmed them. At first, I thought this was a test of my ability, but I realised over time that this came out of their reluctance to take responsibility when problems arose. It was a trait that showed up in strange ways, like the time a young female student came with a problem. It proved to have a simple solution.

'Sister, can I talk to you?'

'Yes Rosie.'

We sat in Papuan silence on my verandah, the quiet that precedes talking.

'My boyfriend wants to sleep with me,' Rosie began.

'How do you feel about that?' I asked, my mind clambering around for a culturally appropriate response.

'I know it's wrong.'

I tried to discover if this meant she was tempted or it was customary to comply.

'Can you tell him you're not going to do this?' It was not allowed on a Christian mission nor was it wise for a young nurse in training.

'No sister, but if you tell me I'm not allowed to, he will stop asking me.'

I duly told her she doesn't have my permission to sleep with him and she left smiling to inform him I'd forbidden it. If only all life's problems were solved this easily.

As expatriate nurses, we found joy in small delights, like the aroma of freshly baked bread wafting through the mission's shop door. We'd tuck into the shared meat on feast days after it was lifted from a pit of coals. The penance on these occasions were the speeches.

'And now Sister Audrey will make a speech,' proclaimed the most senior man present, usually the bishop.

I will? I'd raise my eyebrows in surprise, before I remembered that raising one's eyebrows meant yes in local body language. I'd stand up to make up a speech about whatever came into my head first and everyone listened, which was another surprise. I became accustomed to making inane speeches at the drop of a hat.

During the wet season, my intense dislike was reserved for the toads that leapt into existence and became a pathway hazard, especially at night. If I avoided treading on one, it was sure to jump up my legs, and I learnt to lift my feet well off the ground between steps, prancing home like some Andalusian show horse. The usual tropical creepy crawlies and nasties lurked ready to ambush any unsuspecting new blood. One morning an ants' nest materialised in the turned-back sheets of my bed, in the time it took me to have breakfast and return to my room. Another day I woke to the curious gaze of an emerald green frog clutching to the outside of my mosquito net, just short of my nose. It's as well I'm not a screamer.

I also spent some weeks recovering from a bout of an obscure strain of hepatitis, and despite the prophylactic antimalarial drugs, I suffered occasional bouts of malaria.

Going to the beach to snorkel above the coral seabed was an afternoon pastime in my first year. I had an amusing hat like an umbrella with its spokes attached to a band that sat like a halo around my head. I wore this and a loose-fitting dress for swimming and caused some amusement. My swimming days finished after I snorkeled over a cavernous black hole. I was close to the shoreline and had not expected such an ominous void to open beneath me. Cold water hit my stomach and I freaked out – I almost became a screamer. My imagination was working overtime and I felt I'd swum over the gates of Hades. Who knows what was down there? I was somewhat ashamed of my overreaction and didn't tell anyone about it.

With colleague Cynthia and students at Wedau wharf.

When I arrived at Dogura, the hospital was run by locally trained nurses and an Australian missionary nurse, Lesley, who oversaw both the hospital and school of nursing. She'd done this faithfully, with energy and skill for about 14 years and was trying to withdraw to work on a particular project with a national nursing team in the capital city, Port Moresby. No replacement had been found and it was three years since Lesley gave notice of her intended move. I became principal of the School of Nursing somewhat reluctantly, and my first move was to hand over the running of the hospital to the local nurses. It was time for them, and for me, to take on more responsibility. It was somewhat like being thrown in at the deep end after years of splashing around in the shallows of nursing management. It was sink or swim time, and I discovered I could swim. The senior hospital nurses took up the challenge and within a short time, the standard of care stabilised. Previous tutors had taught them well.

The language in this area of Papua was mainly Hiri Motu, but Papua New Guinea has the highest level of language diversity in the world according to ethnologists. With 850 distinctly different languages across the country, Tok Pisin had developed as a 'lingua franca' as an English-based creole language. Only about 2 per cent of the population spoke English, but we taught in English and all the people on the mission spoke a simple English. For all that, we were a multicultural group of eleven expatriates; British, Australian, Canadian, Indian, Sri Lankan and at one point, French. The campus was full during school term with about 300 girls at Holy Name High School swelling the numbers. Between terms, the population shrank and I would usually take a holiday over the Christmas break.

Over those weeks I would return to Perth and be asked to promote the work of Save the Children Fund in a few talks and on the radio. One result of this was a long article written by a Perth journalist for the 1983 autumn edition of the charity's magazine. It was titled, 'A Busy Day for Sister Audrey', and it gave a true account of many events rolled into one day using some poetic licence. I've included several of them in this account. The journalist observed that my life and work at St Barnabas School of Nursing brought 'long periods of duty, new challenges and sometimes excitement'. She said I needed the wisdom of Solomon, and I would have added 'the patience of Job and other biblical measures of ability'. I suspect many nurses who work overseas must rise to new clinical and life events and find, as we did at Dogura, the best way to come through some of them is to develop a strong hide, have a sense of humour and, essentially, goodwill.

A few more tales – both amusing and sad

The age-wrinkled Papuan shuffled along the path between the hospital and the shop, muttering numbers to himself. John was a man with a purpose and he was heading for the student nurses' dormitory. I was told he had served in the navy years ago, which may explain why John was wearing a fading naval blazer with pride each time he appeared out of nowhere. His mental state would vary, and his stays were never long enough for an assessment. Left alone, he was fine, but interfere with his focus or direction and he became agitated and aggressive. I heard the cry go up from the girls as they chased him out of their dormitory. He was not happy, and neither were they.

'Sister Audrey,' they complained later, 'he was stealing our pants again.'

I was walking back from buying bread at the shop when I noticed three male nurses arrive from the hospital to persuade John to move away. The distant muttering of numbers increased to erupt as a defiant cry of '99!' Numbers seemed to be John's only way to verbalise, perhaps the result of a stroke or other trauma. At this point, we tutors discovered that our laboured teaching on managing disturbed patients had yet to be integrated into practice. The lesson on how to defuse situations like this went to the winds, and the nurses' basic response took over. They tackled John to the ground and fell onto him until he disappeared in the scrum. From under the crush came John's defiant cry of '99!' He gave in, and after a meal and overnight stay at the hospital he shuffled down the hill to Wedau and places unknown.

This event has stayed with me because it upset me and showed me how much needed to change. In later years I saw a similarly agitated client outside a Perth mental health unit. The emergency team spent half an hour trying to settle him down before using a similar, but safer technique. As in many developing countries, care of the mentally unwell was primitive at worst and under-resourced at best. I've never wanted to practise in this nursing specialty.

In light of this last incident, we were delighted when an Australian psychiatrist turned up at Dogura unannounced and offered to give a lecture. The students returned to their desks in the heat of the afternoon somewhat reluctantly. I hoped the doctor would use simple terminology and sat in my office next to the classroom with my ears straining. The students were as quiet as mice and I was impressed that this expert was holding their attention so well. Later that day I chatted with Linda who was their tutor for the subject.

'That went much better than I'd expected.' I said, thinking I'd been unfair in assuming both the level of the doctor's language and the student's attention span. 'They seemed to be listening.'

Linda roared her wonderful belly laugh. 'Steven told me there was an enormous rat walking along the top of the wall above the blackboard, and every time it moved they thought it might fall onto the doctor. Their eyes were fixed on the rat!' And I joined her laughter, which probably raised our endorphin levels and at least that was good for *our* mental health.

Our evening hours were spent writing lesson plans for the next day's teaching. The national nursing curriculum had changed the year after Lesley left and we were barely keeping ahead of the units with our preparation. I was on a steep learning curve on several fronts, but we coped quite well. I learnt how to write lesson plans, develop exam questions and write multiple-choice questions. There was no Mr Google to help us and we relied on our personal teaching books, the hospital's small library and our professional knowledge.

Another of my learning curves was a house building project. A piece of land was allocated by Bishop Rhynold Sanana to build another staff house.

It was on a headland overlooking the ocean and would have been a prime piece of real estate in another world, and If It hadn't attracted lightning strikes. I was glad of the hours that I'd spent as a child tagging along with my father looking at house plans and 'helping' with some of the lesser building work. I was to be the chief architect and project manager and Jason, the local handyman, the builder and assistant project manager. In reality, I dealt with the logistics and payments and Jason told me what he wanted, but didn't always get. We had many conversations at cross purposes, and I caused much gossip and consternation by demanding an indoor toilet. The house was built approximately as I'd ordered, including the toilet. Lightning never hit me and having a kitchenette and toilet in the same building did not make me sick.

To live here on my own was self-indulgent and a great puzzle to the Papuans, who would never countenance living alone. But it kept me sane, I think. I was able to get away for a break less often than others, mainly because I felt it was more important to let the expatriate nurses have some time-out. Having my own space enabled me to retain a measure of normality. Or so I thought until I returned to Australia, and was told I was 'a little strange' during the time I was readjusting to the pace of home.

Linda has since told me how many laughs she was given by listening to my explanations of world events with handyman Jason in the school's library. Newspapers were delivered to the School of Nursing library for all to come and read, and Jason was keenly interested in the outside world. How do you simplify world politics for someone who lives in a place where there is no telephone, poor radio reception due to the barrier of the Owen Stanley Ranges, and an irregular delivery of newspapers? My luxury purchase was the *Women's Weekly* magazine that arrived each month from Alotau. Once I'd finished with this magazine, I'd pass it on to the staff and so it travelled on. Eventually, someone on a health patrol spotted these treasured publications in a hamlet along the coast. I dread to think what people made of this superficial window into 'civilisation'.

During my first year at Dogura, my colleagues were Canadian Linda, sent by Cuso International, and Cynthia, an English midwife posted by Voluntary Services Overseas. They were quietly delighted that I was, at last, going on a mother and baby clinic patrol. These took several days and most included some hard walking in rugged terrain, teetering across bridges made of fallen logs and all manner of challenges and discomfort. Mine was going to Rabaraba about 30km along the coast and then inland where we would spend the night. I set off with two local nurses, travelling the first leg by boat. As we chugged past the isolated palm-lined beaches, the sea below was alive with fish and corals and out to sea a giant manta ray leapt out of the waves spreading its six-metre wingspan to land with a mighty splash. My heart sang at all I saw. Then one of my shoes fell overboard; it was a mistake to take them off.

'Never mind sister, you can have mine.' And I completed the patrol in a pair of rubber thongs (flip-flops). Two days later we returned to Wedau, moored the boat and climbed the hill to Dogura.

'How did you go, Audrey?' Cynthia was intrigued to know how I'd coped.

'Have you eaten? Come and have a coffee,' said Linda.

At times these villages were so short of supplies that the nurses would forfeit their own food supplies of rice and tinned fish so that the mothers and children could eat. My clinic patrol happened at a time when the gardens were producing.

'I had bacon and eggs for breakfast!' I enjoy telling them this. 'And mosquito nets at night.'

I told them about the first night in the mountainside village, where I slept with the girls in a small thatched hut built on stilts above ground. We slept on grass mats and I could hear the hum of thirsty mosquitos and snuffles of foraging pigs below. We washed upstream and used the less-than-private toilet downstream. On our return to Rabaraba I was introduced to the local store owner and his wife, who lived a more comfortable life in a concrete house. I stayed the night in their spare room in a proper bed, and the wife insisted on serving a hearty breakfast. I tried not to gloat as I told Linda and Cynthia this, but their faces told me they felt I'd somehow cheated in an unspoken competition in patrol hardships. They had much harder routes to travel up steep hillsides and across deep ravines. Later we laughed about it and visitors were regaled with the story of my easy first patrol. I avoided the patrols with steep climbs, because I knew my exercise asthma would slow us all down.

These regular hinterland clinics mostly provided antenatal and baby checks and people would walk for hours to attend. Malaria and malnutrition were often the underlying causes and we needed to watch out for signs of tuberculosis. But mostly the diagnoses were treatable. PNG's health service provided two practice handbooks, an orange one for diagnosis and treatment of adult conditions and a blue one for children's health. Nurses and doctors could not deviate from these medical bibles. They had limitations, but generally were safe systems for remote area practice. Some years later I was involved in the writing of something similar for West Australian remote area nurses.

Occasionally a more significant illness would present itself and we'd need the child and mother to travel to Dogura. They would either return with us or walk, as there were few suitable landing sites on the well-vegetated steep terrain. People's patience as they waited to be seen was a noticeable contrast to the Aboriginal health clinics I'd experienced in the Kimberley. There we needed to work quickly, because the clients were unwilling to wait for long. There was also a contrast in the behaviour of the children. I loved the Aboriginal children who were very affectionate and would climb all over me. But the Papuan children ran away from me, and this was hard to take.

'Why are they so shy of me?' I asked the Papuan nurse.

'They think you're a spirit because you're white with light hair.'

'Am I a good or bad spirit?'

'A good one.' That was a relief.

I would need to be careful how I approached the children in these more remote places where they saw few white people, especially blondes. Word must have gone out that I was benign, so the children trailed behind me, still very shy and chiming out that spirit name in my wake.

Sorcery was rife along these coastal villages and I was aware of a sense of evil at times during those three years. I once was woken at night with a great sense of foreboding and lay in bed praying for God's protection. The next day I approached one of the local nurses.

'Was something going on in the village last night?' I asked, noting her surprise and hesitancy before she replied.

'There was a death feast. How did you know?' I told her how I had sensed it in my spirit. She understood and began to open up to me about some local customs.

A few other significant events during those years are worth mentioning. One was the eclipse of June 1983. The name for this in Tok Pidgin was Mun-bin-hittim-Sun, and as with many pidgin words was clarity itself. I kept my tee shirt of this occasion until it was threadbare. There was a national push to educate people about the moon passing over the sun and not to watch it with the naked eye. It was still an eerie experience of daytime darkness and I understood the dread and superstition that it could evince.

Occasionally an expatriate missionary would decide to retire to a village where they'd developed close connections. One such priest lived on a small remote island some hours away from Dogura. The family who cared for him asked for a sister (nurse) to visit and check his health. I set off with the crew of the mission launch, MV *Maclaren*, remembering to keep my shoes on. Three hours further along the coast, we headed out across the open sea. I soaked up the sights of flying fish travelling beside the boat, more leaping giant rays and the pink coral fish busy about their lives below in the deep blue tropical water. The underwater world became clear as we approached coral reefs and sighted land. My lips were salty from the spray and I drank from my water bottle as we anchored. A small canoe paddled out to greet us. I scrambled into the dugout with my medical bag and 15 minutes later we were on the shore of the most idyllic island, walking up a path lined with red bougainvillea and tall coconut palms to a two-storey concrete house.

Father John was a tall, sparingly built man over 80 years old, or so he appeared. I was there about an hour and found him interesting to talk to, but unwell. I could see that people were fond of him, looked after him and he was an accepted part of the island's family. I gave him an injection of anti-biotics and more pills and had lunch and a cup of tea with everyone before returning to the launch by canoe. Father John would die there, and this was his choice. He knew he would never survive nor be happy back in his homeland England. I heard later that Father John had sent urgent messages several times to the archbishop in Port Moresby to come to give him last rites. On the third occasion, Archbishop Hand left the island saying, 'Make sure you're really dying next time.' Or so the story goes. A Port Moresby taxi driver who once drove us up the hill to the bishop's house, called the archbishop 'Number-one-man-belonga-God'. Perhaps this was pidgin for archbishop, but it made our day.

The root crop taro is the staple diet for the people of the area and Wedau had an ancient culture that included irrigation of their taro gardens. This was a fascination to anthropologists, as I was told by Mimi Kahn, an American anthropologist living with a village family. Mimi's wise village mother would send her to visit us at the mission every so often, telling her, 'You need to keep a connection with your own people.' I came to know Mimi a little better and we corresponded for a short while after I left.

Wedau's irrigation channels ran from the local river, which would shrink to a trickle every dry season. At these times food became scarce. The root vegetable taro was vital for their survival and the whole area was known as an area of subsistence living. With 500 people living at Dogura during high-school terms, the mission decided to build a small dam to sustain its water supply during droughts and not drain the village supply. The opening of the dam was a time for celebrating, as was every church festival and feast day. To me, taro tasted like soap and I couldn't like it even when it was cooked with generous amounts of root ginger. My staple diet became rice cooked in coconut milk and tinned meat or fish. Green vegetables were the soft tips of pumpkin vines bought at the local Saturday market. We groaned with desire for an ice cream and headed straight to buy one whenever we visited Alotau.

In 1982 the diocesan council decided Dogura would host a fair on the feast day of St Barnabas. Word went out to coastal and inland villages that the main attraction would be a traditional dance competition. This caused great excitement and preparations began. I was impressed by everyone's ability as they tackled the logistics for this event. The isolation had bred interdependence and all worked together, knew their roles and each competing group catered for their own needs. The competitors and families arrived from long distances, travelling on foot from the mountains and coastal villages. At Dogura, a brush fence was erected around the oval with each village contributing a section.

On the day of the fair, the arrival of the dance groups was preceded by the sound of drum beats and rattling nut anklets. The cicada shrills were drowned out by the drumming, and the village dogs steered clear. We watched the dance group pass the mango trees, skirt the west end of the cathedral and enter the arena, a central grassed acreage. The dust rose as they padded out their dances and the grass, pandanus leaf or tapa cloth skirts rose and fell in rhythm to the bouncing bare breasts of the women. The men strutted like peacocks displaying their feather headdresses and wearing strips of tapa cloth to cover their bare essentials. Tapa cloth was seen more commonly in Oro Province and was made from the bark of a local mulberry tree. The villages have their own unique designs and many years later I hung a large one on my wall at home. Dancing went on all day, and much betel nut and lime was chewed and spat. Betel nut juice can cause mouth cancer, and the streets in the towns were stained from the expelled juice.

The dance and whole event was fascinating, not least because we spotted the bishop's comfortably built wife dancing with her village group, having shed her Mother's Union tee shirt. Leaving the dancers to practise and compete all day, I joined the student nurses to help peel vegetables for the obligatory feast.

'No sister, that's wrong. You have to peel them this way,' one said demonstrating the way their mothers had taught them. There was no arguing either way worked; their way was the correct way. Safety was ignored as we all wielded our sharp knives in very effective, but more dangerous ways. Meanwhile, the men were organising the mumu or underground oven. This involved digging a pit, filling it with hot coals or rocks, adding the pig and vegetables wrapped in leaves, then burying the whole lot for hours so it cooked slowly. Delicious.

As the day wore on, we mingled with visitors and enjoyed buying a few items from the side stalls erected by the high-school girls and village people. Finally, the bishop and Mrs Banks, the head mistress of the high school, announced that everyone had won, which was a wise decision, given that Dogura is an old tribal battleground. Everyone was happy, and a little later we gathered for the feast of roast meat and vegetables. Visiting dignitaries were served first, then the men, then the women and children. As expatriates we were allocated a place higher up the pecking order than the rest of the women. I wasn't very comfortable about this, but I was also hungry and my stomach won. A few villagers lingered for the week, the mission shop made a roaring trade and then Dogura returned to business as usual. The place felt dull and quiet after the buzz of the St Barnabas Day Fair.

By my third year, I knew I needed to decide whether to stay or go. I'd seen people stay away from their homeland for too long, only to find they couldn't readjust or find satisfying work. I didn't want this to happen to me. I was asked by Helen, the missionary who coordinated the Anglican Health Services in the country, if I would replace her. This followed the untimely death of the Papuan man she had groomed to replace her when she retired. It was tempting, and I felt privileged to have been asked, but had reservations. I also thought it was time for a local person to fill the role. I sought the counsel of a godly Franciscan brother and eventually decided not to accept. The sense of guilt remained for some months because I knew there were only a few other options. But I also knew that things generally turned out for the best when decisions were made after prayer and wise counsel. I understand two Australian missionary nurses based in Popondetta took over the role and a few processes changed. Helen retired to a house she'd built close to her adopted Papuan family in Wanigela, a small village in Oro Province.

As for my role in Dogura, a replacement had been offered by the British Voluntary Services Overseas. While he settled in, I decided to visit along the coast and then travel to the highlands to visit friends I knew from Derby, Australia. This leads me to my final story.

It's about my visit to friends Jenny and Gary and their two small daughters, who were living in Telefomin, inland from Wewak in the province of Sepik. This was a Baptist mission planted in the wildest of places, and Gary was a pilot with Mission Aviation Fellowship, a worldwide service. I knew them from my years in the Kimberley when Gary was working for Dick Roberton to increase his flying experience and hours in readiness for work in PNG. It was a joy to see them again and get a better understanding of their lives.

Telefomin is on the edge of wild, densely forested mountains. The people were still unsophisticated and wore very little, despite the cold. The men wore the most amazingly shaped gourds to protect their penises. Jenny and Gary's innocent little daughters referred to this part of the male anatomy as a 'treeness'. It was difficult not to stare at the versatility of shapes, but most things gain a sense of normality when you live among them long enough.

Papua New Guinea was, and is a notoriously dangerous place to fly. There was a saying – 'There are rocks in the clouds'. The weather could change rapidly bringing dense cloud cover into the flight corridors between the mountains. Airstrips were clearings on slopes close to ravines, and some were very scary. MAF was popular and often the only means of transport in these more remote areas. Flights on some lesser known air services were unsafe due to maverick or burnt-out pilots. Lesley, the previous principal of the nursing school at Dogura, had once disembarked from a journey and walked the last 50 or so kilometres rather than fly with the pilot, who she believed was flying too dangerously. I thought this was an overreaction until I had been in the country long enough to understand.

All this information became relevant on the day I travelled with Gary to a new mining site deep into the hinterland. We flew at 10,000 feet or below and wound our way along valleys and over primeval forests. I was seeing God's Earth as it was before time began and I almost expected to see dragons and prehistoric monsters circling below. It was awesome and frightening. If we went down here, no one would find us. My admiration for the work of MAF increased. At the open cut mine site my heart sank. The devastation and scarring to the earth and forest laid bare the unthinking greed of corporations and humanity. It was a rape of the earth and the beginning of the end for this whole region. Maybe the people benefited in material ways, but it was hard to imagine how this was better. I flew home from that visit with a heavy heart.

Leaving Dogura was sad, but I went with a readiness for the next chapter in my life. I flew to Darwin and then directly to London. There, Maree's parents met me and I stayed overnight at their home in Wimbledon. Maree was a volunteer teacher at Dogura and her parents had worked on a leprosy island mission off Hong Kong. Frances and Max were in England on furlough from Kenya, and Frances collected me from Wimbledon. As we walked to the train I complained, 'Do we have to walk so fast?' I had a lot of adjusting to do. My mother's local Anglican church made a great fuss of

Frances and Max, and I confess to feeling somewhat put out that no one realised how I'd been in far more challenging places. But then, I didn't tell them either.

The effects of my years in PNG were written in my diary notes on my return to 'normal life' in Perth.

I now appreciate public transport, orderly queues, fresh meat, salad, ice cream, un-melted chocolate and hot showers. But it's terrible to be wearing proper shoes again instead of sandals. I find myself using simple words of one syllable and avoiding idioms. I can sit through a long silence with comfort. I raise my eyebrows as body language for agreement. I continue to point with my chin. When greeting two people I say, 'Hello two'. I'm learning not to put my feet on the coffee table and not to smell the milk before I pour it. I still chuckle at remembered phrases used by students, such as maternal morality instead of mortality (death). And I smile at the beauty of some remembered explanations; 'Family planning is like planting coconuts. You must have spaces in between, so they can grow.'

I value my Dogura years for the people I grew to love, the things they taught me about honesty in expressing feeling, their sense of community and enjoyment of simple things. I miss the beauty of the place.

Reflection

We can achieve much in our human strength and with our natural talents, but with God we can do so much more. I could not have lived and enjoyed these years in Papua New Guinea without God's guidance and strength. There are many Bible verses that remind us that God is involved in all we do. Here are two favourites of mine.

'The joy of the Lord is your strength.' Psalm 28:7

'Commit to the LORD whatever you do, and he will establish your plans.' Proverbs 16:3

Twelve

WHATEVER NEXT?

Mostly it's best not to know
What's coming in on the tidal flow
with its flotsam and jetsam of daily life.
Oh no! I cry, not more strife.
*

Waves of wonder wash at my feet,
surges of interest flow and retreat.
I gather some, and the let some go.
I ride the highs and then sink low.
What comes next? Best not to know.

I'm sitting in the Dome Cafe in Albany on the coast of Western Australia. The south wind is blowing off the melting ice cover of the Antarctic and it's time for a very hot coffee, a flat white.

'How many chapters to go before your book is finished?' asks my writing buddy, Sheryl.

'I'm into the last 20 years or so and I'm hesitating,' I reply as I sip my coffee and watch the clouds scuttle across the rooftops.

'Why?'

'They were strange years both personally and professionally, but I'm not sure how interesting they will be to others.'

'It'll leave a big gap if you don't say something about them.'

'That's true. Maybe I can tell you bits and you can let me know what you think?'

'Alright.'

'Here we go then.'

⌒

In 1984 I was readjusting from my years in Papua New Guinea and trying to fit back into Western culture with all its materialism and skewed values. Re-entry shock. I felt I'd entered the domain of George Orwell's novel *Nineteen Eighty-Four*. We weren't yet subject to the level of government surveillance and propaganda he described, but I felt very controlled after the freedom of the last three years. This feeling faded as I succumbed to the lure of comfortable living and conformed to social expectations.

I was 40 when I entered the scary realms of home ownership, a mortgage and longer-term government employment. My foray into home ownership wouldn't have happened if school friend Leslie hadn't led me through the process. I was shaken when bank interest rates rose to an all-time high of 17 per cent, but by then I was earning a good income. My home ownership was a relief to my friends who hoped I'd settle for a while. It also meant I could retrieve my few scattered possessions from their spare rooms or garages. Whether or not all this meant I was settled was a moot point. I'd chosen to live in Cottesloe, a seaside suburb in Perth because I loved the ocean. It felt less like living in a city. Coming home from work, I'd inhale the briny sea breeze as I reached the top of Salvado Street that ran down to my two bedroomed unit 50m from the beach. The air temperature was cooler than inner Perth by about 10°C in summer and I was lulled to sleep by the sound of waves spilling onto rocky shores. In winter, I battled against the wind during my daily walk after work. In summer I joined the early morning walkers, but not the swimmers. The local Anglican church, St Philips, gave me a spiritual home and I was a happily occupied for several years making a home for myself and reconnecting with old and new friends.

This was an ideal place and time for my Mother to visit from England. It was her first and only visit, one that she'd talk about for years. It was a particularly hot summer for Perth that year, but Mother took it in her stride. In later years she would remind me of the heat saying, 'We could have fried an egg of the bonnet of the car!' When her mental health deteriorated, she insisted we'd actually done this. She continued to imagine me in that unit although I moved several times.

The years around 1984 also marked the beginning of further professional development. I completed a Child Health certificate mainly because I'd worked with children in community health and overseas. I thought it wise to get the qualification. I was unaware that I'd been offered an earlier place on the course. The telegram took three weeks to get to Dogura, by which time I'd left PNG.

My next role was with the Health Department's Children's Day Care team in Perth. I enjoyed travelling around the day care centres to check the children's health and development. Children would innocently volunteer amusing and worrying tales about their home lives, and I met children and parents from all socio-economic backgrounds. Our team met each week and included a developmental paediatrician, social worker and allied health specialists. These meetings were valuable times for problem solving and support. I was disappointed to learn some years later that the team had been absorbed into an area of the Children's Hospital in a departmental restructure. It was better placed in a community setting.

Back to the Kimberley

My habitual restlessness struck after two years and I needed a new challenge. I'd long since decided it was futile to complain about health management unless I was prepared to become one of 'them' and involve myself in some of the decision-making. I had three nursing certificates, 20 years' nursing experience and began studying for a nursing degree at Curtin University. I could continue to study part-time externally or return to full-time study at a later date. I deferred and eventually completed my degree in 1990.

I applied for the position of Deputy Director of Community Nursing in the Kimberley, the place that always drew me back.

'Ah, Audrey, we were waiting for you to apply,' said the interviewing nurse, much to my surprise. I smiled, thinking, *Pity no one told me.*

Within a month I was up, up and away into middle management. Derby's humidity and chorus of frogs greeted me, along with my new boss, Mick. I'd managed to arrive during the Wet again. Mick, the nursing director, had organised a helpful orientation for me and then he let me work out how best to fulfil my role. I enjoyed travelling the region as I managed and supported the remotely-placed community health nurses. I soon discovered it was wise to visit the main nursing bases at least once a month; the regular communication helped to address any issues quickly. My schedule was to travel for two weeks and remain in and around Derby for two weeks. I was responsible for maintaining and improving the skills of the nursing workforce and arranged staff development workshops in collaboration with others. I enjoyed all this, learning from my mistakes and growing in confidence. Over time, I learnt to handle staffing issues more firmly and accepted that I couldn't please everyone. I re-accustomed myself to the constraints and demands of our government bureaucracy, but I missed the independence I'd experienced in Papua New Guinea. My Canadian friend Linda was well qualified and experienced, and she was employed by Kimberley Health for a year. It was a treat to have her on 'my patch' for that time.

It was good to reconnect with friends like the Robertons, and I attended the Anglican church with them. This was across the road from the People's Church that had nurtured the rekindling of my faith in 1975. The church building was nicknamed 'The Gothic Garage' but it was more garage than Gothic. We were a mixed congregation of Uniting Church and Anglican faithful, and the service rite depended on which minister was presiding. Each Sunday we'd ask one another, 'Are we Uniting or Anglican this week?'

We didn't mind which one it would be. Dick Roberton would pound out the hymns on the small organ and we'd sing in varying levels of tunefulness and gusto. No little boy made a cicada shriek and no preacher said, 'I may be wrong, but I know I'm right.'

⁓

I was concerned about the working conditions and hours of the nurses based in Aboriginal communities as both were onerous. Several times I drove or flew into remote nursing stations to extract exhausted, troubled nurses. My own experience in Papua New Guinea had taught me that working in a remote location for too long without a break can make a person reluctant to leave. This reluctance was an indicator the person needed a break – before they lost all perspective. The stress of long hours could sometimes be exacerbated by outbreaks of community infighting and violence. The violence was fuelled by alcohol and most communities became alcohol-free sites. But there were unscrupulous taxi drivers who would deliver to the gate for an exorbitant price, or people had a secret stash outside the community boundaries. Groups would binge drink and be a danger to themselves and others, and the nurses were called after hours to stitch wounds on very drunk and uncontrollable clients.

At times the nurses needed to remove themselves from the community for a few days. Once I flew in and brought out a lone nurse who was showing signs of excessive stress. Withdrawing a service was not permitted without higher government authority, but as a desperate acting director, I withdrew the service and then explained it. I listed the reasons in ten dot points for head office in Perth advising them of the change. I was grateful for the help of the Director of Nursing at Halls Creek, so that we were able to very quickly recommence the service as a daily fly-in, fly-out nursing service. The community's health workers provided after-hours help and did this very well. The strategy worked and was so cost effective that it continued for about two years. At the time it stirred up a hornet's nest of consternation with the Perth-based heads of departments. However on the positive side, it influenced greater inter-departmental collaboration for some of the more troubled communities.

The Kimberley was not unique in these incidents, as I heard when I attended National Remote Area Nursing conferences. By the 21st century all nursing posts were required to have a minimum of two nurses and some places have a police presence. The advent of new technologies also helped.

There's a saying that if you drink the water of the Fitzroy River you will return to the Kimberley. I wasn't aware of drinking the muddy waters of that local river, but I expect some of it seeped into my pores. I certainly returned a few times and loved travelling the region. It was a privilege to have access to so many places. I continued to jump at the chance of spending weekends with Mike and Dasee and their family on their boat. It had a canopied deck that reminded me of the one in the 1951 film *The African Queen*. So that's what I called her, even though no one else knew the film. Old friend Jock would have known it, but sadly he died a few years earlier. We'd leave Derby jetty from the boat ramp and Mike would judge the tides in King Sound so the boat's hull would clear the rocks but still avoid the fast-running water cascades of the incoming tide. We'd head to a little-known cove up the sound where Mike had set up a small campsite with a food safe and a few stores. It was an enchanting place, apart from having to watch out for a wandering saltwater crocodile. There was a freshwater stream nearby that fell down a small cliff to create a shower, and a shady beach in front of some low trees. The few people who knew of Gugeri's camp would always restock the safe when passing and not abuse the privilege. During the day the family would fish from the boat while I enjoyed watching the bright colours of the fish in the waters below. A rifle was always kept on board in case crocodiles or huge sharks threatened us. At night we sat on the beach eating damper and fish cooked by Dasee, then slept in our swags in a row at the top of the beach, with Mike opting to sleep on the side closest to the ocean with the rifle. Outback chivalry.

The dunes and clifftops held unmarked graves from ancient shipwrecks. Mike would hunt these out and report them to the museum in Perth. These hunts led to our anchoring in some remote coves along the coastline around Cone Bay where we waded ashore. Walking around the pools left by the ebbing tide, I looked up at the surrounding cliffs. The silent stillness oozed a tangible peace and I felt I'd entered a moment in history untouched by humanity. The essence of creation infused all around me and I stood stock still in awe, feeling like an intruder. It was a special moment that met my spirituality and resonated with a similar moment I'd experience while flying over the primeval forests in the New Guinea highlands.

Further south in Fremantle they were cheering large yachts and hailing Australia's winning team of the America's Cup. I was winning much more by being on a launch in the King Sound.

An Incident

Two groups of staff units (flats) were built in Derby in the late 1970s and I moved into one of these during 1987. I'd previously been in a house, but it made sense for a family to have it. The units were comfortable but lacked a phone. These were installed after my frightening incident one night. I woke suddenly to see the dark outline of a man leaning over me. The room was black and I couldn't see more than his outline. I like to believe that he was reaching for the small radio on the shelf behind me on the bedhead. I discovered that my 'flight or fright' response was to fight, which may surprise people who know me. I was out of bed in one swift leap; my hand instinctively bounced around the top of my bedside table searching for a weapon while I faced off my foe. I shouted, 'Get out!' in a voice that surged into my throat from my gut, deep and gravelly and not at all like my usual voice. The intruder turned and fled. I ran after him in a fury before having the presence of mind to stop at the open glass sliding doors.

I paced around the lounge and spent the rest of the night awake, too scared to go outside and alert my neighbour. At dawn I ventured out, walked two doors down to my boss's unit and we reported it to the police. I stayed the next two nights with the Roberton family. The intruder remained unidentified, and Laurie, the Aboriginal health worker was cross that I hadn't the foresight to ask him to look for footprints. He could have tracked the intruder and probably identified him from his footprint. This experience left its mark in my dreams for some years and made me even more safety conscious. It also taught me something new about my nature. And telephones were connected to several units, although not all.

'Goodness, Audrey. This was quite an experience along with all the work responsibility,' says my attentive friend in the café.

'Yes, I suppose it was, but I learnt something about myself through the intruder incident. With work, most of the nurses were competent practitioners and I got to see the whole region from the view of its indigenous communities. In hindsight, this was a unique and privileged way to see that part of Australia.'

'But you left eventually.'

'Yes, but a little later. Mick, my boss developed health issues and was transferred to Perth to work at head office. That's when I discovered senior management was easier than middle management, although it took more responsibility.' I laughed.

'When you left the Kimberley where did you go next?'

'I asked for a transfer to Perth in 1988. You know, I miss the people of the Kimberley and the whole region was a great place to live and work, except during the build up to the Wet. I'm glad I was there during those years. It's much more populated now and I worry about the damage to that amazing eco-system and wilderness.'

We sat in silence for a while. My coffee was cold. I went to order another.

I'd become more interested in organising and running workshops for nurses and occasionally for other health staff. Community Health nursing had a staff development department based in Perth that organised and ran courses for its nurses across the State. I asked to be transferred to this section and it was here that I grew my adult teaching skills under the guidance of experienced educators. I continued my university studies. My great joy during that time was to work with a talented colleague, Jenny, in the development of the Remote Area Nursing Course. She led the project and I was the one with the field experience. The curriculum and modules were all published and used through Curtin University's Nursing Faculty. We were very proud authors. Had we been more forward-thinking, we could have used this project as part of a postgraduate master's degree.

Over the next five to ten years major change marched through all government departments, trampling on many tried and true systems with its hobnail boots. Or so it seemed to me. New vocabulary hit the fans and changed the function and abiding ethos of public health. We came to know words like restructure, downsize, outsource, redeploy, redundancy and outcome-based everything. The Australian Nurses Federation (ANF) was involved in protecting nursing jobs and conditions but were unable to do more than advocate for a fairer deal. The changes continued. The two worst outcomes were the demise of the Community Health Service as we knew it and the redeployment of too many skilled senior community health nurses into the general nursing workforce, away from their specialty. I was one of them. I was angrier at seeing colleagues moved into other fields of nursing or encouraged to retire early with barely a thank you. They'd committed 20 to 30 years of their working lives intervening to prevent diseases from taking hold of people and populations. As we packed up our offices at Swan District Health Service, only one person came to say goodbye. The only other farewell visitors we had were those who wanted us to hurry so that the redecorating could begin. It was devastating. Added to this, I was now considered 'Management' by ANF and outside their support. I was considered one of 'them', in spite of my union membership. We were powerless. The public health system was overwhelmed by the hospital system and we couldn't warn the public. By the time the effects showed in the State's morbidity statistics it would be a *fait accompli*. Administrators had taken control of the system and the front line was left to deal with the reduced service and face the public.

I married in 1993 as all this was unfolding. We met at a Church Missionary Society weekend. My husband-to-be was there to set up the sound system and record the talks. I was there to mix with like-minded people and hear the speaker. I soon noticed I had a shadow as Tim sat next to me at most meal times. He followed me up after the weekend and I thought I simply had a new friend. The attachment deepened and we married about six months after our first meeting.

The bride

Meanwhile, my agitation increased about the changes to our health system, and I would go home and complain to him. 'The way this is being done is heartless, and the people have no idea what's going on. It'll have happened before anyone realises what they've lost.' Then we'd take the dog for a walk, which usually settled me down and let Tim unload his day.

My anxiety levels soared, my energy levels plummeted and my sense of humour disappeared. Meanwhile, my husband had his own issues and despite our common faith, the marriage eventually foundered. This may not have surprised others, but it did me. The shock shivered through my body when he told me he'd made a mistake in marrying me. One issue was my inability to have children, which we'd discussed at length before we married. He was younger than me. More problems arose or were left unexpressed; counselling didn't help and within three years of marriage we separated. I'd not met my husband's expectations of marriage and I couldn't stay. Ten years later we divorced.

The pain of this loss was akin to a death, only the body would reappear. I felt I'd let everyone down, including myself, and shamed myself before God, the church and my friends. I'd become another divorce statistic and felt worthless, angry and grief-stricken in never-ending waves of emotion. I cried, I ranted on my long walks and began to wonder how damaged our Western society was, given that so many people were going through separation and divorce. Over the coming ten to twelve years I fell into a cycle of clinical depression. Each time I fell into 'The Pit' I'd pray: 'Here we go again Lord, please walk with me.' I'd imagine myself as Daniel in the lion's den, protected from the jaws of the beast. This image helped for a while and my depression was not apparent to most people. I was able to withdraw during the bad times and could function reasonably well at other times.

Eventually I realised I needed wise human help and found a good counsellor. In time, I emerged a stronger, more knowledgeable person with more understanding of those who experience anxiety and depression. The accumulation of stressors from my workplace, marriage and early life experiences played a part in those dark episodes. In recognising my need for help I was able to heal and return to a more balanced attitude to life. The good times are no longer blocked by the unhappy ones.

I sat in the café with Sheryl. She has listened without interruption to my rising voice recounting events and feelings.

    'I see why you weren't sure about how to write this. Time for a break?'

    'Yes, I think so. I'll work on the rest and read it to you on Friday.'

    We talked about other things, checked if it was still raining and made a run for our cars.

    'See you on Friday.'

    'See you on Friday.'

Reflection

Life teaches us many lessons and these years matured me in several directions. Some of my responses and reactions were helpful and others not. There are two doves in my garden. One is grounded but otherwise healthy, maybe stunned from a fall. The other sits with her while she recovers and gains enough strength to fly again. It's a safe space for them. I look at the doves and I'm reminded that God's presence was with me as I was tried by life. When we are knocked down he sits and watches over us, waiting for us to recover and flex our wings once more. A friend indeed.

    'I am the Lord who heals you.' Exodus 15:26

    'Cast all your anxiety on Him, because He cares for you.' 1 Peter 5:7

Thirteen

Retiring – or not

Tick tock, tick tock.
We're watching the clock,
We're clocking the watch,
joining the march of time.
Tick tock, tick tock.
Time has flown, if only I'd known
years ago, when time was slow,
that where one's from isn't it,
It's more about 'being' and shoes that fit.

Clocks struck twelve, ships whooped their happy hooters and fireworks flew across Perth's skyline, marking our entry into the new millennium, the 21st century. I was celebrating with friends, and reminded myself that I was to be available and in my right mind in case I was called by work. All organisations and businesses were on tenterhooks, waiting to see if their computer programs would crash as they flipped over from 1999 to 2000. We'd all had to prepare for the worst and have plans in place in case of extended power failure, water pump failure and all sorts of computerised gadgets and machines failed. I was part of the Health Department's Disaster Planning Committee. Our brief was to develop contingency plans for a disaster. I'd found this all very interesting, but as the New Year approached I recalled one possible scenario. It was the failure of a specific area's large sewage pumps. If the contingency plan failed, the result didn't bear thinking about. I'd made an appropriate visit to the Ladies before the clock struck and hoped this particular catastrophe would be avoided. All was well, computerised systems coped and I continued to celebrate with the affluent, forgetting the effluent.

The year 2000 was significant for me in several ways. The Health Department was still making changes and my permanent position in Perth was under threat but not earmarked for redundancy. I'd had enough and decided to move to Albany. I wanted to be closer to the friends I'd known as family for so many years, my old school chum Sheelagh, her husband and two sons. It was Sheelagh's parents who took me in all those years ago in Kenya, during my father's illness.

It took longer than I'd expected to break into Albany's tight job market and I transferred to Public Health in Albany. I also had difficulty finding a house I liked and grabbed the opportunity to buy a block of land in a suburb about 10km out of town. I was excited to be creating my own home using an architect and builder, but I was very naïve about much of the process. The result may not have been as successful without Sheelagh's timely advice and the godly coincidence of my choice of architect and building company. Sadly, the builder went out of business soon afterwards, but I gained a house that won a building award. However, I did get a bit carried away with its size and after three years, I moved into a delightful small house in Albany's town centre. I enjoyed my first Albany home with its view of lush pastures, the sound of cows mooing and the telescopic sight of ships approaching Albany's port. But the move to town proved right and it's hard to believe that I've lived in this smaller house for 15 years; the longest I've remained in one place in my lifetime of moving. This move brought me full circle to where my Australian life began in 1972, and was where I planned to eventually retire.

Perth friends were surprised by my decision to move to the temperate climate of the Great Southern region.

'Audrey, you'll be too cold in Albany,' they said.

'Don't worry,' I joked. 'With menopause and global warming, I'll be just fine.'

My days of being a tropical hothouse flower were over, and if the winter months proved too spartan, I could join the 'grey nomads' and travel to the warmth of the Kimberley for July and August. This plan hasn't happened yet and retirement became a misnomer when life intervened. Life included family happenings, financial security and involvement in my church community.

$\longleftarrow\longrightarrow$

I experienced a small fright soon after moving into my first, built home. An earth tremor rattled through the suburb, something that happens infrequently. It was nighttime and I awoke to the sound of the oil slurping in the bedroom radiator. I jumped out of bed onto the moving floor, ran to grab my passport and purse and came to my senses as I stood outside my front door. Habits instilled in other places had made this flight an automatic response. I looked up and down the hill on which my house was perched, decided I was no better off outside and moved back inside. The tremor subsided and it would be 15 years before I experienced another small quake in Albany.

The following year the wider world was shaken by an event that was not an earthquake but a man-made disaster. This was the terror attack of September 11, 2001. It's burned into people's memories, and like many others I remember where I was when the news broke. It was a rare day when I was late for work and missed listening to the morning news. I was greeted at the office by a cluster of colleagues.

'Isn't it awful?' I was bombarded as I walked through the door.

'What is?'

'Just go and turn on your computer and watch the news.'

They wanted me to experience the same impact they'd known as I watched the screen. I stared in disbelief as the horror unfolded; New York's Trade Centre North Tower was in flames and black smoke was billowing around a gaping hole in the building. Then the South Tower was hit by a second aircraft. The building began to crumble and some of these first pictures showed people leaping to their deaths to escape the flames. It was surreal and I watched fixated. The city streets choked with falling white rubble and a fast-moving stream of ghostly dust-covered people fled from the descending debris. I looked up at my colleagues waiting by my office door and our work suffered for the rest of the day as we repeatedly checked the news and talked together.

The 9/11 attacks provoked the United States into declaring a war on terror, beginning with the Iraq War, and we entered an era of increased terrorism perpetrated by Islamic fanatics. The Australian public were advised 'to be alert but not afraid'; mostly we were naïve and ignorant. Australia's alliance with the USA drew our military into wars in Iraq and Afghanistan, and for the first time since the Vietnam War, families grieved the death and injury of loved ones through war. War wounds and post-traumatic stress have marred many lives since.

Having been raised in an insecure country I quickly readjusted to security checks at airports. I've grown used to being frisked, scanned and sniffed by dogs seeking out explosives. Everyone is suspect and I fear George Orwell may have been right after all as our lives are cumulatively monitored. My father once told me that science fiction is where we get to see our future. He was right.

Retiring

The years surged on at an alarming rate and I've retired four times. The first time was to exit the Health Department in 2001. This lasted about two weeks. I was immediately offered an interesting role in the region's General Practitioner support organisation. The next retirement was at age 60 to release my superannuation and reduce my working hours. My whole being was screaming to pull out of the regular workforce. But I had very little superannuation as a latecomer to the scheme and I needed to make it last as long as possible. I worked for the GP Network for six years with a few breaks between contracts. I began to weary once more of watching government policies shift health costs and powerbases, and felt the role of nurses was still being devalued in anything but acute care. I became eligible for the age pension six months after turning 64, and continued to work part-time before retiring a third time. My colleagues began to refer to me as 'the wise old owl upstairs', which I took as a compliment. Climbing the GP Network's office steep staircase kept me fit and I told the chief executive officer that if I was still working at 70, they'd need to put in a chair lift. As it happened, I was working in a different capacity when I turned 70 and the lift was not needed.

The Big Surprise

I involved myself in a broad range of roles at my church during my 60s. I enjoyed building up the church's community and supporting others in leadership. It became a time of new learning and then a new career and calling. This part of my spiritual journey has marked out my later years and was entirely unexpected. It was less unexpected for others, and several people over the years had suggested I train for the priesthood. I'd laughed at the thought.

I usually sensed impending changes to my life, but I hadn't seen what had been bubbling along within me for years until it burst out in an unusual experience. I heard an audible voice that I knew to be the voice of God. I imagine I was so slow to understand what I was being asked to do that the Spirit of God resorted to the shout of a still small voice. 'Deacon!' said the voice quite clearly at the back of my head. I was driving at the time and was pleased the road was clear of traffic as I clung to the steering wheel in surprise.

These sorts of spiritual experiences are not often understood or accepted by most people, Christian or not, and I balked at speaking about it for months. I'd not heard God audibly before although I knew this was not a unique event. The rational part of one's brain suggests the voice is an hallucination or a mental emanation, but my inner being told me different. I heard the voice, no matter which part of my brain was tapped into by our Creator.

I sought advice from my minister and so my journey began. I discovered that my role within our church community was very like that of a deacon, and I was being asked to enter the Anglican way of being set aside and affirmed in that ministry. If God was indeed calling me into ordained ministry, it needed to be tested and the Anglican Church has an established process for doing this. This included going through a series of hoops of assessment and discernment and facing a panel of wise clergy and lay people. I received mature counsel and endorsement from the bishop, my home parish and diocesan leaders.

Candidates are also checked out by a psychiatrist and I enjoyed telling my friends I had proof of sanity, which was more than they had. Bishop Allan Ewing and the discernment committee accepted my application and I moved into three years of more learning and assessment. I needed to complete a prescribed level of theological and practical training, and as I've always enjoyed learning, this was a delight. I thought my age would make me ineligible and I'd worried that my divorced status would bar me, but neither did. It was all about discerning the depth of my faith and veracity of my call. It was about being who I was meant to be. I also had life experience to offer, and so a new pathway opened; more steps in my moccasins.

Family Update

Over the years things had been happening within my family. Frances and her husband Max had left Africa Inland Mission and Kenya after 20 years' service and returned to England. Their two adult daughters, Clare and Faye, had both married, and Faye and her American husband had a son, Ryan. I became a great aunt and was able to visit California several times to catch up with Faye and her family. On these trips I visited my dear nurse friend Gilly, with whom I'd trained in Oxford. She was living with her husband and two sons in Connecticut. Gilly also visited me in Perth. Meanwhile, my many cousins had produced further generations and I gave up trying to keep up from such a distance. My mother moved from Lincolnshire to be closer to Frances in Hampshire, England. She became frailer of mind and we realised this when she was certain she'd seen a unicorn. But she still didn't look her age and was physically quite fit, even if she didn't think so. My choice to remain in Australia was not difficult, but I often felt guilty about Frances taking the load of Mother's care and I made frequent long-distance journeys. Compromise comes with choices and nothing is ever fully what we would like, or so I have found and come to accept. I was grateful for Frances' care of Mother and her assurances that I should stay where I was.

Frances

It was especially exciting to have my sister Frances stay with me in Albany for three weeks during one of my retirements. We had a wonderful relaxing time of afternoon drives around the sights and beauty spots of the region, and we both enjoyed simply being sisters again without the call of others on us. Our childhood bond had remained all our lives and we understood one another well, with nothing needing to be explained. She redesigned my little garden and I was happy to go along with most of her suggestions. We had deeper discussions about our childhood and the differences in our experiences.

As it turned out, this holiday was a bonus for us both as her previous cancer was about to emerge in her bones. It had been ten years since she was cleared of breast cancer. After her visit I spent two lengthy stays in Hampshire with her during her long terminal pathway. As it happened, I arrived on my third visit the day before she died in September 2010. She was 69. Her death left a gaping hole in her husband's and children's lives, and in mine.

Mother never spoke of Frances after this, which was how she coped; a mechanism learned over years of loss, I suspect. Mother's memory and eyesight deteriorated but her faith remained firm. She was cared for in a well-run nursing home in Brockenhurst, and Max visited her several times a week. My stepbrothers continued to help with her nursing home fees and I honour them for this. Mother fell and broke her hip and some months later died. She was a month away from her 99th birthday. I became an orphan and the 'last man (woman) standing'. This was a strange feeling and disturbed me more than I realised over the following two years of grieving. Then quite suddenly, it was as if a shadow shifted and I began to feel the sadness lift.

Strolling on

As I grieved Frances, I was occupied by moving towards being made a deacon, which happened in 2012. Going on to be ordained as a priest was another surprise. I began my priestly ministry several months after Mother's death in 2013. I have a lifetime calling and although I have retired, the fourth retirement, I do what I can. Like my parents I look younger than my years (so I'm told) and my hair hasn't turned grey, for which I take no credit as it's genetic. Although my memories of long ago are clear, I find I lose my glasses more often. I hope I never see unicorns like Mother. There are years ahead if I go on to 99, and I suspect God has not finished with me yet. There's still more wear in the moccasins.

Epilogue

The incense swirls heavenward with the prayers and praise of the people who turn to watch the stream of red-robed clergy flow down the cathedral aisle. The thurifer is indeed thorough as he swings the censer with its perfumed smoke forwards, left and right. The woman waiting in the front pew, covers her nose and mouth with her service booklet and the asthmatics in the congregation begin to cough. She would have preferred a simpler form of ordination, but this is the tradition of the Anglican Church in Australia. This part of God's worldwide church is where she's been called by God into lifelong service.

'Who'd have thought it? the Reverend Audrey,' her friends say.

'Better late than never,' says the happy Reverend, and those who know her well agree.

And as she waits, the memories of her lifelong journey dance in her head and heart.

Where are you from? Where are you going? It doesn't matter anymore; it's all in God's hands, and she feels at home.

Lightning Source UK Ltd.
Milton Keynes UK
UKHW011029190520
363484UK00006B/1875